EXISTENTIAL REASONS FOR BELIEF IN GOD

A DEFENSE OF DESIRES & EMOTIONS FOR FAITH

CLIFFORD WILLIAMS

IVP Academic

An imprint of InterVarsity Press
Downers Grove, Illinois

InterVarsity Press
P.O. Box 1400, Downers Grove, IL 60515-1426
World Wide Web: www.ivpress.com
E-mail: email@ivpress.com

InterVarsity Press® is the book-publishing division of InterVarsity Christian Fellowship/USA®, a movement of
students and faculty active on campus at hundreds of universities, colleges and schools of nursing in the United States
of America, and a member movement of the International Fellowship of Evangelical Students. For information
about local and regional activities, write Public Relations Dept., InterVarsity Christian Fellowship/USA, 6400
Schroeder Rd., P.O. Box 7895, Madison, WI 53707-7895, or visit the IVCF website at <www.intervarsity.org>.

Scripture quotations, unless otherwise noted, are from the New Revised Standard Version of the Bible, copyright
1989 by the Division of Christian Education of the National Council of the Churches of Christ in the USA. Used by
permission. All rights reserved.

While all stories in this book are true, names and identifying information in this book have been changed to protect
the privacy of the individuals involved.

Design: Cindy Kiple
Cover image: NAGOMU KATO/Getty Images
Interior image: Frolov Sergey/iStockphoto

ISBN 978-0-8308-3899-8

Printed in the United States of America ∞

 InterVarsity Press is committed to protecting the environment and to the responsible use of natural
resources. As a member of Green Press Initiative we use recycled paper whenever possible. To learn
more about the Green Press Initiative, visit <www.greenpressinitiative.org>.

Library of Congress Cataloging-in-Publication Data

Williams, Clifford, 1943-
    Existential reasons for belief in God: a defense of desires and
emotions for faith/Clifford Williams.
        p. cm.
    Includes bibliographical references and index.
    ISBN 978-0-8308-3899-8 (pbk.: alk. paper)
    1. Faith. 2. Christianity and existentialism. 3.
Emotions—Religious aspects—Christianity. I. Title.
    BT771.3.W55 2010
    239'.1—dc22

                                                                          2010040608

P 20 19 18 17 16 15 14 13 12 11 10 9 8 7 6 5 4 3 2 1

Y 28 27 26 25 24 23 22 21 20 19 18 17 16 15 14 13 12 11

It is not enough to think about our destiny: it must be felt.
—Miguel de Unamuno, *Tragic Sense of Life*

CONTENTS

ACKNOWLEDGMENTS

THIS BOOK BEGAN WITH A CONVERSATION with Rod Taylor during the 2004 Cornerstone Music Festival in Bushnell, Illinois. I was giving talks on Kierkegaard and Nietzsche, and Rod, who at the time was finishing a Ph.D. in English literature at Indiana University, was in the audience. During lunch at his camper, he expressed dissatisfaction with evidential apologetics and wanted someone to explore need-based grounds for believing. He thought I should do it. The book was nudged along by a conversation with Ann Eberhardt, a former student, for whom the traditional evidential arguments for faith did not work. I am grateful to Rod for further conversations, plus Gary Deddo, Scott Erdenberg, Titus Hattan, Kirsten Hildebrand, Christopher McCammon, Ellen Palmer, Letha Dawson Scanzoni, Corey Shenk, Mark Vincent, Linda Williams, several of those whose faith journeys appear in the book, and an anonymous reader for IVP Academic, some for conversations on the topic of the book and some for comments on the manuscript. I also want to thank the people who recounted their faith journeys to me for their honesty and passion. I have changed their names so that they can remain anonymous, but I am indebted to them, both for the part their accounts play in this book and for their personal interactions with me. I also thank Trinity College for granting me a sabbatical to work on the book and Yvana Mols, who replaced me at Trinity College while I was away. I am grateful as well for the opportunity of working in the Bodleian Library at Oxford University while finishing the manuscript.

INTRODUCTION

NEED AND REASON

CHRISTIANS HAVE DIFFERING VIEWPOINTS about the role that the satisfaction of needs should play in acquiring and sustaining faith. Some Christians think that the satisfaction of needs should play little or no role. For them, only reason can tell us that faith is legitimate. Satisfying needs has little or nothing to do with the legitimacy of beliefs. The apologetic tradition in both Protestant and Catholic Christianity stresses this standpoint.

Other Christians think that faith should be acquired and sustained through the satisfaction of needs, for otherwise faith would be barren, disconnected from what matters most to us. Many Christians, in fact, have come to faith because it satisfies deep needs. Some of these Christians regard reason as less trustworthy than need, for reason often leads people astray, especially those who are influenced by the secular culture in which we live. It is better to trust one's needs—not just fleeting feelings or wild desires, but emotional and spiritual needs that all humans share.

Christians also differ on whether emotion is a component of faith. The partisans of reason regard faith as consisting primarily or wholly of assent to the truth claims of Christianity. If this were not so, they say, faith would be as shallow and fickle as emotions are. And like emotion, it would be blind and disruptive.

The advocates of emotion, however, view faith-as-assent as lifeless. It contains no vibrancy, no energy or passion. A rich and lively faith cannot consist simply of intellectual assent. It has to have the emotional depth that Christian virtues such as love, joy, peace, patience and kindness possess. How can mere intellectual assent, they ask, have this depth? And why must all emotions be shallow, fickle, blind and disruptive?

These two dichotomies are connected. Those who believe that faith should be acquired through reason are likely to think of faith as excluding emotion. But those who believe that faith should be acquired through satisfaction of need are likely to think of faith as consisting of emotions, for satisfaction of need involves having emotions.

Two questions frame the discussion of these themes: (1) Is it legitimate to acquire faith in God solely through satisfaction of needs? (2) Does faith in God consist of emotions? I answer that the ideal way to acquire faith in God is through both need and reason, and that faith should consist of both emotion and assent.

The answers provided in this study are middle-of-the-road assertions. They steer between rationalists and emotionalists. Rationalists emphasize reason, and emotionalists emphasize emotion and need. I want to emphasize both. My aim is to defend the legitimacy of acquiring faith through need, emotion and reason. Satisfaction of need legitimately draws us to faith, but reason must be involved in this drawing. More simply, the two basic ideas of the book are the drawing power of need and the certifying ability of reason. Need without reason is blind, but reason without need is sterile.

Other claims about the value of existential reasons for faith occur within the context of these themes:

1. Emotion and need can be trusted for faith in God as much as reason.

2. The negative assessment of emotions by some Christians is unjustified.

3. The remedy for being led astray by emotions is not to distrust emotions, but to develop the right emotions.

4. Christians should cultivate emotions as much as they do commitment and right action.

5. Having the right emotions is necessary for discovering certain truths. Objectivity and neutrality, free of all emotion, are not the only paths to determining the nature of reality.

6. We are not just "rational animals," as Aristotle asserted, but "emotional animals" as well.

7. Apologetics in Protestant and Catholic Christianity has been too evidential. It should be supplemented with existential apologetics, the demonstration that Christian faith is justified because it satisfies certain emotional and spiritual needs.

8. Emotions are part of what makes life spectacular.

Christians need a conception of faith and life that is at least as much need-based as reason-based. To some readers, this focus on need and emotion will seem obvious. "Of course the satisfaction of needs should play a part in one's faith. Who ever would have thought otherwise?" But many philosophers, theologians and lay Christians have, indeed, thought otherwise. To these readers, focusing on need and emotion will seem wrongheaded. Faith needs a more secure foundation than that, they will say. On one hand, they are right: the satisfaction of need should not be the only basis for faith. But one should not throw out the satisfaction of need altogether, for the ideal way to secure faith is through both need and reason.

This thesis applies to both acquiring and sustaining faith. If one comes to faith largely via the satisfaction of need, one should supplement that process with reason; if one comes to faith largely through reason, one should supplement that with the satisfaction of need. So this book is as much for those who have faith as it is for those who are wondering whether to acquire it.

The matters I shall discuss divide Christians not just intellectually but personally. Some people acquire faith largely in one of the ways, and they sometimes have trouble connecting to those who have acquired it largely in the other way. The divide affects denominations and church services as well. Some denominations lean more toward one side of the debate than the other, and church services are sometimes conducted with an emphasis on emotion or reason. Those who gravitate toward one side of the divide feel out of place in a denomination or church service that gravitates toward the other side.

Sometimes the divide becomes a matter of whether one can retain one's childhood faith. Several years ago an acquaintance who had been reevaluating the faith with which she had grown up asked me why I remained a Christian. I answered that I continued to think that there were good reasons for believing that Christianity is true. She replied that she used to think the same, but in college, she had no longer found those reasons convincing. What kept her a Christian at that time, she said, was need. More recently, another acquaintance described how he was having trouble with his Christian faith because the emotional highs he was provoked to acquire during church services later departed. Faith, to him, could not be based on emotions, as they would soon crumble, and since he had no other basis for faith, his was crumbling.

I am going to sprinkle this book with personal accounts of faith. They are based on interviews I recorded, transcribed and edited. In some cases, I asked two questions: (1) How did you get started on your faith journey? And (2) what happened next? In other cases, I asked, What kind of faith are you looking for? To insure anonymity, I have changed the names of those I interviewed.

These accounts of faith journeys vividly demonstrate the interplay of need and reason, an interplay that cannot be neatly demarcated. Theorists may have a clear-cut distinction in mind, but when we look at how people actually come to faith, the distinction gets blurred. There is no precise order in which the appeals to need and reason occur. It is not always reason first and then need, or need first and then reason. The two are often inextricably mixed. So we must keep in mind Aristotle's advice that a theory should not attempt to be more precise than its subject matter allows. My thesis that the ideal way to secure faith in God is through both need and reason will, consequently, have to remain less precise than many theorists would like it to be. In some way or other, the two are needed for a secure faith. Beyond that, we may not be able to specify exactly how the two operate.

These accounts of faith also demonstrate the passion, energy and intense concern that people often possess in their faith journeys. Theorists of faith sometimes neglect this living dynamism, this sheer force of emotion. From time to time, however, they need to stop thinking and look at what really occurs when people acquire faith. This book is, accordingly, both a theoretical account of faith and a depiction of real, lived faith.

Chapter two describes what is meant by "needs" when I talk about faith meeting needs. Significantly, not only are they quite numerous, but they are also interconnected. It is not just the simple "need for God" that is relevant to believing in God, but a complex network of needs.

Chapter three outlines the existential argument for believing in God. In its simplest form, it says that we are justified in believing in God solely because doing so satisfies certain emotional and spiritual needs. This argument must be distinguished from arguments that use evidence to conclude that God exists or that Christianity is true—evidential arguments—and especially so from evidential arguments based on needs or the satisfaction of needs. I shall explain the difference between existential and evidential arguments with special reference to Pascal's approach in the Christian classic *Pensées,* in which he tries to convince people to embrace Christian faith with both existential and evidential arguments.

Chapters four, five, six and seven consider four objections to basing faith on the satisfaction of needs. The first objection states that if believing in God on the basis of need is justified, then so is believing that Invisible George protects us from harm because it is satisfying to believe that he does. In other words, satisfaction of need is no guarantee of truth. The second objection states that the existential argument for believing in God does not specify what kind of God is to be believed in. So if the existential argument is sound, a person who had a need to believe in a God who likes to torture innocent humans would be justified in believing in a perverse God. The third objection is that not everyone feels the needs I say people have, so the existential argument for believing in God never gets started for them. It would work for some people but not for others. And the last objection asserts that some people satisfy the emotional and spiritual needs mentioned in the existential argument for believing in God without using faith, or with a non-Christian faith. Those nonfaith states and different faiths would, then, be equally valid ways of satisfying the needs.

These objections do, indeed, show that by itself satisfaction of need is insufficient to justify acquiring faith in God. However, this fact does not show that satisfaction of need cannot be used at all in acquiring faith. It can if it is supplemented with reason. And it should be, as we are creatures with both needs and reason.

This conclusion is relevant to the question of whether faith consists of emotion, the topic of chapter eight. Emotion, rightly understood, is a legitimate component of faith. Because the satisfaction of need involves having emotion, this conception of faith fits with the thesis that satisfaction of need contributes to acquiring and maintaining faith.

The last chapter, chapter nine, makes three assertions: we should let ourselves be drawn to faith in God by need; we do not always do so; and having emotions is part of what makes life spectacular.

This book is aimed at both professional and lay readers. Though it contains complex argumentation, I have cast it in terms accessible to those with little professional training. It is my hope that both audiences will profit from it.

EXISTENTIAL NEEDS

Most people of faith acquire their faith partly because they feel that it meets what I am going to call *existential needs* and partly because they think that it makes sense or is true. Martha came to faith through these means. From her childhood, she says, she "longed for a true and living spirituality." In learning about Christianity she became aware, "through the songs, the sermons, the Bible studies, Sunday School classes, that a Christian God is one who loves us, is a God of compassion, of caring, of forgiveness." Although it is impossible to separate need from "reason" in her account, both need and reason, in this book's terminology, propelled her to faith. Here is her story, in her own words.

MARTHA: OUT OF DEPRESSION

I grew up in a traditional Protestant church where there was an expectation that you would be confirmed at the age of fifteen or sixteen. To do that you had to go through confirmation classes. Each of us was given a mentor, an older member of the congregation who made sure that we knew answers to questions about Luther's catechism and other things. I wanted it to be meaningful in some way, but I didn't know what that meant.

When I went to college, I met a student who was very

articulate about her relationship with God and Jesus' love—she spoke about her relationship with God in personal terms. I was unfamiliar with that kind of spirituality. My experience of spirituality was more in a corporate setting, in the church, the liturgy, and discussions with other students at the student group I became involved with. This seemed different to me somehow, and I was curious about it. I think there was within me a yearning to understand this, to know God in the same way. I had a sense that things could be better—I don't mean that my life could have been better, because my life was really quite good. It was more a yearning for goodness, maybe a closeness, an intimacy, a sense of peace, a sense of being loved. I'm not exactly sure. There was definitely a desire, but a desire that always had the hope, maybe even the assurance, that it would be fulfilled.

There was also this: the hope was followed immediately by doubt and sadness and concern and a sense that I didn't measure up. I don't know where this was coming from, but for whatever reason, genetics, natural temperament, imperfect parenting, a household with a lot of anger, I was a shy, melancholic, fearful child. And I grew into a quite depressed young woman. My deepest and most authentic emotions were those of sadness and despair. Tragedy was strong in me. It characterized my worldview and gave me my self-identity. These feelings, I have to say, were very profound. They formed who I became, feelings of inadequacy and not being good enough and not being loved. I think I was aware of those things before, but becoming aware of the promise of God's love made them all the more poignant, all the more evident to me. At this time, while I was in graduate school, I was in the midst of a very loving congregation. So it wasn't as if it was a need that wasn't being met among my human relationships.

I was encouraged to talk with a professional counselor, and I did. With her I read a book called *Telling Yourself the Truth*. You examine the kinds of things you are saying to yourself, and your behavior changes as you say different things to yourself. The author is a Christian writer, and the text from which he wrote is Jesus' saying, "You shall know the truth and the truth will set you free." The point is that some things we say to ourselves are lies. They may be things that someone said to us in our formative years, and we persist in saying those things. We can identify that we are saying those things and begin to say other things to ourselves that are true. For me it goes back to the song, "Jesus loves me, this I know." I am a child of God. I was created in God's image. God loves me.

I found that this was very helpful. Those things that I often said to myself didn't have to be. I could change. I could just say outright that those negative things were not true and begin to say other things to myself.

People prayed for me in a group setting, people I knew and trusted, who knew a little bit about my story. This happened probably a few times. At one point in one of our prayer times, the young son of one of the elders broke into the prayer circle, crawled up into his dad's lap, and just sat there. He lay back and sucked his thumb. The elder commented to me, "This is God's heart for you, that you crawl into God's lap." That kid knew his dad was going to accept him and hold him. I knew, though, that it was not what I felt, not toward my earthly father, and not toward God, either. It was something I needed, but which I did not have.

One Sunday afternoon at 4:30, I think it was, I was cleaning my apartment and praying under my breath, maybe in response to something on the radio—it was a Christian talk show, but I was only half listening. Suddenly it was as if God said, "It's enough. It's enough. Your longing for me, your yearning for me and desiring to know that I love you is enough. It's done. It's over. You've been dealing with depression long enough. Do you not see it?" It was as if lights were turned on, in a split second.

This experience occurred about eight years from the time that

I was a junior in college. So it was a long period of saying, "I'm a child of God but do not feel fully loved." In that moment I was filled with joy, a kind of emotional release.

I went to work the next day and my boss said, "You're different. Something has happened. What's up with you?" I told her. I was working for a Christian nonprofit organization at the time. What I was feeling inside was evident to someone else. Somehow my carriage was different, my disposition, my facial expression. I felt freer, more at peace.

Up until then I had had a very strong sense of myself as being someone who was melancholic and tending toward depression. I knew nothing of happiness, even at a superficial level, much less joy. But afterward I had the freedom to focus on what I was doing and the people I was working with. Before, I was always taking my temperature, trying to figure out what I was feeling—"Am I measuring up, am I feeling sad now?" I wasn't saying these things to myself anymore. I wasn't nagged by self-doubt, feelings of inadequacy, and sometimes paralyzing sadness. I no longer characterized myself as a naturally depressed person. I was able to read the promises of scripture and say them, sing them, with the sense, "This is true. This *is* true."

TWO KINDS OF NEEDS

We have dozens of needs, but only some of them are relevant to believing in God. This chapter describes such needs. I am not claiming that everyone feels all of these needs, though later I will claim that many people feel some of them and that many more can come to feel them or become aware that they feel them to some degree. Feeling at least one of the needs is all that is required to make the need-based argument for believing in God of interest to someone.

Needs can be divided into two categories: those that are self-directed and those that are other-directed. Self-directed needs are aimed at getting something for ourselves, such as cosmic security and meaning.

Other-directed needs are aimed either at the good of others or simply at what is good, such as expressing love or praise. When we satisfy an other-directed need, we do, indeed, get something: the satisfaction of having met a need, plus perhaps a desire to satisfy it in other ways. But what we get from satisfying an other-directed need is not the object of our aim in satisfying the need, as it is in satisfying a self-directed need.[1]

This distinction challenges the common idea that those who believe in God because of need do so only for the satisfaction of self-directed needs, that is, that they believe in God only for what they can get from believing. Sigmund Freud thought this. He claimed that everyone who believes in God does so because they think they will acquire security from a strong cosmic father. This claim has two parts: everyone who believes in God does so because of need, and this need is self-directed. The reality, however, is that believing in God sometimes results from other-directed needs. This point will play a role in my answer to the second objection to the existential argument for believing in God, which says that the argument does not specify the nature of the God who is the object of belief.

I am going to call both the self-directed and other-directed needs "existential" instead of religious needs, partly so as not to prejudge the question whether they can be satisfied by faith in God and partly because they deal with what is of ultimate concern to us.

SELF-DIRECTED NEEDS

Cosmic security. When we are not thinking of the uncertainties of life, we feel secure. We will not be washed away by a tsunami or tossed about uncontrollably by a tornado. Our jobs are relatively safe, and even if we lost them, we could find others. We trust the nation in which we live to provide security of various sorts. But when the thought of death comes to mind, we quickly avert our attention from it, knowing that if we dwelt on the thought of our own deaths, we

---

[1]Merold Westphal describes this distinction in "Religion as Means and as End," in *God, Guilt, and Death: An Existential Phenomenology of Religion* (Bloomington: Indiana University Press, 1984), pp. 122-37, and "Prayer and Sacrifice as Useless Self-Transcendence," pp. 138-59. He refers to certain other-directed activities as "useless" because they are good as ends, valued for their own sake and not a product of self-concern or valued as a means to an end (pp. 138-39).

would get a knot in the pit of our stomach. We need a larger security than jobs or nations can give.

Imagine that on an occasion of reflective solitude, thoughts of our final end catch us, unbidden, and a cosmic uncertainty overtakes us. Suddenly the thought that God will make things right, come what may, occurs to us. A tornado may ravage our homes, we may lose our good health and our job, but God will make it so that we do not sink into nothingness. This is the feeling of cosmic security. We feel protected no matter what—not that we will never undergo hardship, but that even if we do, we will be okay.

Beyond the grave. We cannot possess cosmic security unless we also believe that we will live beyond the grave. Imagine, again, that we are alone, thinking of the rest of our life. When we were young, the rest of our life was an indefinitely extended future—we could not see the end then. Now that we are older, perhaps over forty or fifty, we can picture the rest of our life as a definite span. When we picture this finite span to ourselves, we ask, "Is this all there is to life—my life? I began a certain time so many years ago, and I will end only so many years from now. How can this be?" We feel that we must remain living or else life would make no sense. Nothing would matter in the long run. Nothing now would have any point to it. Or so we tell ourselves. And this means we need to know that we actually do keep on being conscious in some way after we die.

Heaven. But it is not mere existence that we want after we die. We want a certain kind of existence. We want one that is free from the hazards of this life, free, that is, from misfortune that is out of our control—from the ravages of the cancer that may slowly kill us, from the misshapen body that embarrasses us. We want rest from the constant effort needed simply to pay bills. And we also want a different kind of rest—from the effort required to battle temptation and from the emotional pain that our parents caused us by their unjustified criticisms or lack of love. We do not want any more anxiety about the future. We want an inner contentment that is not punctured by bouts of depression.

Perhaps it would be more accurate to call this need for heaven a longing. It is less a conscious need than a wistful yearning. We feel it vaguely instead of explicitly, and fleetingly instead of continuously. Perhaps, even, we do not recognize it as a desire for heaven. It is simply a craving for something different from what we now experience.

Goodness. It is not, however, just something different that we crave. We want goodness, as there is little of it, it seems, in this life. This is the goodness that springs from a vision of an ideal life, one that is full of virtues such as kindness and generosity, and full of glad cooperation among individuals of different races and convictions. We sometimes dream of what the world would be like if this goodness really existed. Our dream is indicative of a deep-seated desire for this goodness, and it makes us wish, perhaps even hope, for a time when true goodness is visible in everyone. Our desire is partly other-directed and partly self-directed, for we desire that everyone be good, and we picture ourselves being like everyone.

A larger life. The craving for something different from what we now experience is also a desire for a more expansive life. We want to know more about the hopes and dreams of our acquaintances, the workings of long poems or large engines, the physics of the beginning of the universe, the sociology of subcultures. We want new experiences—of fascinating places, grand landscapes, magnificent works of art, beautiful prose, new people. We do not want to experience these simply to see how big a pile of experiences we can get—that would be miserly. We want to have these experiences because we want to have certain emotions—awe for the grand landscapes, magnificent works of art and beautiful prose; appreciative understanding for the emotional life of our acquaintances; exhilaration at discovering something new about the beginning of the universe or the workings of culture; moral awe at observing goodness. Our desire for these emotions is a desire for a richer life, one that has a wider array of the emotions we regard as significant.

To be loved. There are, of course, other ways in which we crave that our life be richer, one of which is to be loved. "To love and be loved," wrote Richard Rolle in *The Fire of Love,* "is the delightful purpose of all human life."[2] It is not selfish or egocentric to want to be loved—truly,

---

[2]Richard Rolle, *The Fire of Love,* trans. Clifton Wolters (New York: Penguin, 1972), p. 121.

that is, and not in order to be admired or to enhance our reputation. We want to be loved by our parents at first, then by friends and later perhaps by a spouse. We want to be known and understood, trusted and valued—not only for what others legitimately get from us but for our own sake. It gives us a sense of security when we are loved, though not of the same sort as the cosmic security I mentioned earlier. Rather than protection from debilitating harm, love gives emotional security.

Meaning. On occasion we imagine what our life would have been like without love. We would have been a wreck. We would not have been able to go home at night to an empty house or to one with discord and discontent. We might have tried to find relief from a loveless life by some sort of escape activity. Or we might simply have numbed ourselves to the hollowness we feel. Though we could survive without love, it would be a dreadful existence. For without love, we would have nothing to live for. And without cosmic security or life beyond the grave or goodness, we would have nothing to live for either, we feel. We crave meaning. If we do not find it in the satisfaction of these basic needs, we look for it elsewhere, sometimes with a vengeance.

To be forgiven. When we realize we have looked for meaning in places it cannot be found or in places that give only a transient or vacuous sense of meaning, we want to know that we are still loved. A sense of having gone astray afflicts us. It may be sharp, in which case we agonize over our wandering heart, or it may be subdued, in which case we are merely uneasy about it. In either case, we need to know that we will not be rejected because of having lost our way. If we think of this need in the context of God, it turns into the need to be forgiven by God.

OTHER-DIRECTED NEEDS

It may sound odd to call other-directed needs "needs," for we commonly think of needs as springing from self-concern. But it is legitimate to do so, for we would feel impoverished if we did not meet them, just as we feel impoverished when self-directed needs are not met. It is a different kind of impoverishment, but it is impoverishment nonetheless. This fact shows that we do, indeed, feel other-directed needs, even though we may not get anything for ourselves when they are met.

To love. We do not want just to be loved, but we also want to love. We want to care deeply about a small number of persons, to know them deeply and to trust them. It gives us satisfaction to give something to them or to do things for them. We also want to be compassionate toward those who are in difficult or miserable circumstances.

Awe. Awe is a combination of feelings: "solemn and reverential wonder, tinged with latent fear."[3] We feel awe when we encounter something majestic in nature—the vastness of the ocean's horizon, the colossal size of a nearby mountain peak, the amazing complexity of the human brain. Perhaps we do not experience fear toward the brain's complexity, but we do when encountering the largeness of oceans and mountains. They make us feel small and vulnerable: something could happen to us that we would not like. The fear is only latent, though. What is explicit is the feeling of wonder: how can anything be so large? We do not see anything like that in our front yard or in our commute to work. So when we first catch sight of the horizon or the peak, we cannot help gasping.

We also feel awe when we encounter people who are stately and magnificent, such as royalty whose bearing is princely, or when we witness a flawless performance of a technically complex and difficult task, such as the playing of a long and intricate piano piece.

There is another kind of awe we experience less often but one that is just as real. I am going to call it moral awe. When we read about someone who has sacrificed herself for the sake of another or who has spent a lifetime working for the good of those who can never repay her, we feel moral awe. When we personally observe an acquaintance do something heroic, we feel the same kind of awe. Perhaps, even, we feel this awe when we notice small acts of kindness, so unexpected that they catch us by gratifying surprise. Here, too, is something grand—a different kind of grandness than that of mountains or regal persons, but grandness nevertheless. It too is worth a gasp of glad and reverential wonder.

When these three kinds of awe are directed toward God, they in-

---

[3] *Oxford English Dictionary,* 2nd ed., s.v. "awe."

crease in intensity, for God is larger than a mountain, more magnificent than a head of state, and possesses a more expansive goodness than any human.[4]

Delighting in goodness. We fall in love and take keen pleasure in the goodness of our beloved, not just the personally attractive features, but the moral goodness our beloved displays. Or we become a parent and are glad when our child shows honesty and courage. Our delighting in goodness is like delighting in beauty or noncompetitive play: we do not have a motive for doing so other than that we like the beauty and play and recognize their value. We aim our delight at nothing other than the goodness of our beloved.

Being present. We like to be with those we love and with those who love us. The point is not to be doing something together, but simply to be in the other's presence. Merely sitting quietly with someone we love makes us glad and contented. Doing so is partly self-directed and partly other-directed. We like being in our beloved's presence, but our attention is focused on our beloved, just as awe and delight in goodness are focused on their objects. We are both present with our beloved and present to him.

Though the need to delight in goodness and the need to be present with another are components of love, we can direct these needs toward people we do not know. We might delight in the goodness exhibited by a stranger or, after having been alone for a time, we might want to be present with the first person who comes along.

Justice and fairness. We are sensitive to the pain and suffering others undergo, in particular the suffering that is not due to any fault of their own. A young acquaintance has been in and out of hospitals for a variety of reasons and now has been diagnosed with pancreatic cancer. He will die in agony or become dulled and insensible with painkillers. We wince at the unfairness of one dying without being able to experience all of the good things he wants to. Everyone should have the same chance, we feel. Similarly, no one should be murdered or tortured or raped or op-

---

[4]Rudolf Otto includes awe in his conception of the feeling of *mysterium tremendum*, though his conception of awe is tinged with dread and the feeling of "something uncanny." See his "'Mysterium Tremendum',' in *The Idea of the Holy* (New York: Oxford University Press, 1958), pp. 12-24.

pressed by a tyrant or deprived of basic rights. We cringe at the horrific evil that people inflict on others—the genocide in far-off countries, the slavery in our own, the murders by a serial killer. We want to see justice done, and we want to see the victims compensated. This, of course, involves life beyond the grave, as very few to whom appalling and ghastly evil has been done are compensated to any degree before dying.

These thirteen needs are what I have in mind when discussing need-based reasons for believing in God. They may not be the only needs that are relevant to believing in God—I am not supposing that the list is complete or that I have captured all of the subtle and fertile desires involved in them. They do, however, capture the richness of our spiritual personality better (and with more precision) than a shorter list. N. T. Wright has four needs on his list: "the longing for justice, the quest for spirituality, the hunger for relationships, and the delight in beauty."[5] And Freud, as is well known, has just one: cosmic security. Of course, just one need is all we require to begin considering whether need is a legitimate basis for acquiring faith in God. Still, it is better to have the panoply of needs in mind, for that represents human nature more accurately, and it makes discussion of need-based reasons for believing in God more inviting.

NEED AND DESIRE

Someone may ask, what makes all of the thirteen items needs rather than desires? If they are described as longings, as some writers do, would not that mean that they are more like desires than needs? And if they are desires instead of needs, would not that undermine their force for believing in God? The reasoning would be, "I believe in God because I want to." And this has a good deal less persuasive power than saying, "I believe in God because I need to."

The usual distinction between need and desire is that needs are felt more intensely than desires. The *Oxford English Dictionary* defines *desire* as a "feeling or emotion which is directed to the attainment or possession of some object from which pleasure or satisfaction is expected."[6]

---

[5]N. T. Wright, *Simply Christian: Why Christianity Makes Sense* (New York: HarperSanFrancisco, 2006), p. x.
[6]*Oxford English Dictionary*, 2nd ed., s.v. "desire."

Need, however, is defined as an "imperative call or demand for the presence, possession, etc., of something."[7] Using this distinction, we would say that for certain people some of the thirteen items are needs and some are desires, that for others all are just desires, and that for still others some or all are neither needs nor desires. This is because the thirteen items are felt with varying levels of intensity.

There is another way to think of needs, desires and faint longings. This has to do with their object and not their intensity. What is common to needs, desires and faint longings is that something would be acquired if the needs, desires or faint longings were satisfied. The object of the need, desire or faint longing is relevant to what one believes and how one lives, not the intensity of one's affective state. What matters is the object of the affective state, that is, what we would lose if the need, desire or faint longing were not met, not the strength of the feeling for the object. In the present case, one would lose being connected to God. So it does not matter whether the thirteen items mentioned in the existential argument for believing in God are thought of as needs, desires or faint longings. It is the significance of what would be lost that counts in determining their role in coming to believe in God.

Of course, the intensity with which people feel the thirteen needs does affect whether such needs will actually impel them to believe in God. It is not quite true, as stated above, that the intensity with which the needs are felt is irrelevant to whether or not they can be used to acquire faith in God. One will be more likely to acquire or sustain faith in God via the needs if they are felt more intensely. And one will be less likely to be propelled to faith in God if they are felt less strongly. So it matters whether they are actually felt and to what degree. It matters, that is, to their efficacy in producing faith, though not to their relevance to the faith. Chapter six explores the objection that not everyone feels the needs mentioned in the existential argument for believing in God. For now, I shall assume that at least some people experience some of the thirteen either as needs, desires or faint longings. And this assumption is enough to start off the existential argument for believing in God.

---

[7]*Oxford English Dictionary*, 2nd ed., s.v. "need."

3

THE EXISTENTIAL ARGUMENT
FOR BELIEVING IN GOD

Iꜰ ᴡᴇ ᴀꜱᴋ ᴘᴇᴏᴘʟᴇ ᴡʜᴀᴛ ᴛʜᴇʏ ᴡᴀɴᴛ their faith to be or what kind of faith they are looking for, if they are looking for it at all, we find nearly always that they want a faith that fits both need and reason. They want to have certain needs satisfied, and they want faith to be true to reality. This, at any rate, is what I have found when I ask people what they would like their faith to be. I also have found that some people appeal to need more than reason, and others appeal to reason more than need, as the following two accounts show. Michael is a professor in his late forties with a Ph.D. in bioorganic chemistry. Andrea is a music teacher in her late twenties.

MICHAEL

As a person whose interest has been in the sciences for quite some time, fairly early I understood that these systems of thought made sense out of large swaths of life and experience. At the same time, I also saw that a great deal of what the physical and biological scientists that I worked with pursued with their lives engendered inconsistencies. The scientific worldview made plenty of sense out of certain realms of experience, but that didn't necessarily translate into the lives of those scientists.

People who were tremendously successful in their scientific lives led relatively or extremely broken lives when it came to the relational sphere. It almost seemed that the more fervent they were in what one might term *scientism*, the notion that scientific ways of approaching the world provided the deepest and most thorough-reaching sense of meaning, the more likely they were to have broken relationships. So one thing I was looking for in a worldview was something that didn't undermine the scientific approach and at the same time allowed for a greater sense of cohesiveness across the board.

The second thing I was looking for in faith was this: somehow out of my upbringing I came away with the notion that the least satisfying or least valuable life is one that communicates that it is "all about me," that my existence should be focused on myself. So whatever I would do, the choices I would make would have to lead me to be a part of something that was bigger than myself. When it's only about me, the story becomes pathetic and tiresome and narrow. But when one imagines that there might be a story that's about something bigger and grander than just me, then dimensions open up that otherwise would never have been perceived.

And not because I went looking for them, but because I was willing to entertain these possibilities, these were the things that I found. I found ways of seeing that complement science, and evidence that it is not just about me, that there are grander stories than the self-absorbed one that any one of us could write.

ANDREA

When I was a child, probably five, maybe a little bit younger, my mom told Bible stories to me. One night there was a thunderstorm, and I was scared. I needed something or somebody to be in control. I knew that my mom couldn't control the thunderstorm. She shared with me the story of Jesus calming the storm when the disciples were in the boat. That made a lot of sense to me, and that's when I first believed that God could give me peace. That's what I wanted, something to comfort me. So initially it was my need to feel secure that scared me into calming that fear. Later on it was more of a need for a friend. I needed someone who understood me completely and knew all the parts of me but still loved me.

Sometime in college faith became more intellectual. I had questions. Some of my circumstances shattered the idea of somebody being in control or being a perfect friend. It seemed as if faith couldn't be that simple. I wondered about the character of God and whether he was truly loving and all-powerful. I wondered how God could allow certain circumstances in my life and in the world.

The passage in the Bible that meant the most to me then was the one when many of the people who were listening to Jesus left because he was saying difficult things. He turned to the disciples and asked them, "What about you?" And they said, "You have the words of eternal life. Where else are we going to go?" For me it was not a matter of having answers to all the questions or understanding everything completely, but believing that Jesus had the words of eternal life.

That brought me almost full circle to when I was a child. Even though my questions were a lot bigger than thunderstorms, in the end the same thing was true—he is in control. He has the words of eternal life, and I needed to rest in that. That was enough even though I didn't understand. So it went back to a more simple faith.

Andrea's movement toward faith can be construed as an existential argument: I believe in God because I need a cosmic controller, peacegiver and friend. The second thing that drew Michael to faith also seems to fit the mold of an existential argument: I believe in God because I need something bigger and grander than myself so that life will not be pathetic, tiresome and narrow.

THE ARGUMENT STATED

The basic form of what I am calling the existential argument for believing in God is this:

1. We need cosmic security. We need to know that we will live beyond the grave in a state that is free from the defects of this life, a state that is full of goodness and justice. We need a more expansive life, one in which we love and are loved. We need meaning, and we need to know that we are forgiven for going astray. We also need to experience awe, to delight in goodness and to be present with those we love.

2. Faith in God satisfies these needs.

3. Therefore, we are justified in having faith in God.

I am calling this argument "existential" partly to differentiate it from evidential arguments and partly to locate it in the broad tradition of existentialism. I say "broad" because the argument is clearly not pessimistic, despairing and atheistic, as are the writings of the French existentialists Albert Camus and Jean Paul Sartre. Their brand of existentialism broods on the dark features of the human personality—anxiety, aloneness and conflict—which by themselves do not lead to faith in God. The existential argument for believing in God, however, focuses on features of the human condition which, it says, involve needs that can be satisfied by faith in God. Though both it and the French existentialists describe deep human emotions, they go in different directions, one toward God and the other away from God.

The existential argument for believing in God fits better the existentialism of Søren Kierkegaard, a nineteenth-century Danish philosopher. Like Camus and Sartre, he probes the recesses of the mind, and like them, he finds darkness and despair, evasion and deceit. But his aim is to prod people toward Christian faith. For Kierkegaard, the point of uncovering subtle ways we hide from God is to move us into not hiding from God. And Kierkegaard finds needs that he thinks can be satisfied through faith. We are sick at heart and need to be free from the torment it produces. We sorrow, are burdened with care, labor in futility, and need rest for our souls. We have lost our innocence and need to be saved from the sharp distress of guilt. We can have these needs met, Kierkegaard declares, by accepting Jesus' invitation to give us rest: "Come here, all you who labor and are burdened, and I will give you rest." This invitation goes out "along the highways and along the lonely ways," calling out to those who need inner tranquility.[1] Though Kierkegaard does not formalize his statements into an argument, he seems to be putting forward one that is like my existential argument for believing in God. My argument is more in tune with Kierkegaard's existentialism than with that of the French atheists.

It should be noted, though, that adopting the existential argument for believing in God does not make one an existentialist, for there are other distinctive claims that existentialists commonly make. Existentialists, both Christian and atheistic, stress the need to take responsibility for one's life choices and not uncritically let the "herd" or the Christian "crowd" determine one's life path. They focus on individual freedom and authenticity. These existentialist claims are, indeed, compatible with the existential argument for believing in God, but one can adhere to the existential argument for believing in God without adhering to these distinctive existentialist claims.

As we have seen with Andrea and Michael, those who use the satisfaction of need to justify faith in God usually do not appeal to all thirteen of the needs mentioned in the existential argument. In fact, they usually appeal to no more than two or three. The impact of the argument would be stronger if it appealed to more or all of the needs at once, but the question is not the argument's impact but its validity—that is, whether any of the existential needs can be used to justify faith in God. Some people may feel certain needs more intensely than they do other needs mentioned in the argument, as did Andrea and Mi-

---

[1]Søren Kierkegaard, *The Practice of Christianity*, trans. Howard V. Hong and Edna H. Hong (Princeton: Princeton University Press, 1991), pp. 16-20. For explicit statements by Kierkegaard that his aim is to prod people toward Christian faith, see his *On My Work as an Author* and *The Point of View for My Work as an Author*, in *The Point of View*, trans. Howard V. Hong and Edna H. Hong (Princeton: Princeton University Press, 1998).

chael. These people will find that the argument has more impact with respect to these needs. But different people may feel the other needs more intensely and so find that a version of the argument mentioning those needs makes a stronger impression. But no one need is more vital than another with respect to the legitimacy of the argument.

THE STRUCTURE OF THIS BOOK

This book is built around the structure of the existential argument for believing in God given above. In this chapter I will discuss the overall initial appeal of the argument and show how the argument differs from evidential arguments based on need. In the next two chapters, I will consider whether the conclusion of the argument can be inferred from the premises. The first two objections say that it cannot. A third objection denies the first premise: some people do not feel the needs mentioned in the first premise; a chapter deals with this question. Then I will consider the second premise ("faith in God satisfies these needs"), which a fourth objection does not deny, but says that some people find that nonfaith states and other faiths satisfy the needs mentioned in the first premise, which invalidates the argument for them.

THE CHRISTIAN GOD?

Before looking at the existential argument, I want to say something about whether the "God" it conceives of is the Christian God. To answer this question, we need to determine what conception of God fits the needs mentioned in the argument. The needs include the need for cosmic security, the need to be loved, the need to experience awe, and the need to delight in goodness. So the question is, what conception of God must a person have to believe that faith in God satisfies these needs? The evident answer is that God must be conceived of as a being who is able to control what happens to us so as to ensure our ultimate safety, loves us thoroughly and unreservedly so as to meet our need to be loved, is magnificently great so as to satisfy our need to experience awe, and is perfectly good so as to meet our need to delight in untarnished goodness.

Does the Christian God possess these characteristics? The answer, I believe, is yes. In Christianity God is conceived as one who can ensure that in the end things will turn out okay no matter what happens to us now. We may be tossed about by economic or family catastrophes, but God can secure a life after death that is free from such catastrophes. In Christianity, too, God is one who loves thoroughly and unreservedly, sometimes in a motherly way and sometimes in a fatherly way (though Christians through the centuries have focused mostly on the latter). We may have been betrayed or ignored or otherwise not loved as we need to be by those around us, but God does none of these. In Christianity God is so extraordinarily large and complex and creative that one can hardly help feeling awe toward such a being. It is an awe that exceeds what we feel when standing on the very top rock of a mountain or learning about the neurology of the human brain or first glimpsing the Grand Canyon. In Christianity God is perfectly good. Though we may delight in the goodness we observe in those we encounter, God's goodness prompts even more delight, according to Christianity.

So the needs mentioned in the existential argument for believing in God can be met by faith in the Christian God, and have actually been met by such faith in numerous people, as the stories in this book demonstrate. If the existential argument works at all, it justifies belief in a God who is personal, has certain abilities, loves, is "large" and is good. It does not, however, justify belief in all the features of the Christian God, such as that God is triune or exists necessarily. But then it is not meant to justify belief in a full-blown Christian God. All it is meant to do, and all it can do (if it can), is to justify belief in a "merely Christian" God.

I will take up the question whether faith in the Christian God satisfies the existential needs better than any other means of satisfying them in chapter seven. But presently, let us look at some features of the argument.

THE INITIAL APPEAL OF THE ARGUMENT

The existential argument for believing in God is initially appealing to a number of people, as it was for Andrea and Michael. They experience some of the needs mentioned in the argument, they want those needs satisfied, and they find that faith in God satisfies the needs. They are propelled toward faith for the same reason that anyone is propelled toward satisfying needs, namely, because having an unfulfilled need is unpleasant.

There remains, of course, the question of what would satisfy a given need. Some cases are obvious, such as cosmic security. In other cases, it is not so obvious, and reflection and perhaps experimentation may be necessary to find out what would satisfy the need. But a remedy, once found, is highly attractive. Faith can fall into both categories. Some people react to encountering their need to live beyond death and free from the defects of this life by saying, "Ah! Faith in God would satisfy that need." It does not occur to them that a natural condition or activity could satisfy the need. Faith in something supernatural is the only thing that would work. And so they take on that faith.

Others try nonfaith ways of satisfying the needs before settling on faith as a way of satisfying them. In trying to fill the hollowness that afflicts them on weekends, they may surf the Internet or indulge in games and entertainment that get them through to Monday. During the week they watch television for hours, read cheap fiction and surf the Internet even more. These activities, they realize after some years, are not enough. They need something that is decidedly not frivolous.

Or, more subtly perhaps, they want to live more expansively. They travel to places that are meaningful to them—a small village in rural Mexico or Peru, in which they mix with the residents, or the Colorado Rockies, where they immerse themselves in natural beauty. They find new friends and spend time communicating with them via the Internet or by texting. With their travels and new friends, they find a deeper satisfaction, and they do, indeed, live more richly. But something still gnaws at them. Their restlessness returns and they want something more, though at first they are not sure what that something more would be. What they want, they finally decide, is to feel a permanent contentedness without sacrificing their zest for new experiences, and they discover that faith in God can give this contentedness.

An analogy highlights the appeal of the existential argument. Suppose that one evening I am feeling particularly lonely. It occurs to me that I have kept pretty much to myself lately. I have not done much with my friends or talked much on the phone or written many letters. So I decide that I will do these things.

This thought process is a little bit like an argument:

1. I need to assuage my loneliness.

2. Doing things with other people will assuage my loneliness.

3. So I am justified in doing things with other people.

I do not, of course, consciously reason in this step-by-step way. I do naturally what my need to alleviate my loneliness requires, almost by instinct, just as I eat when I am hungry or try to get warm when I am cold. Still, what I go through is something like an argument. In a similar way, I may have faith in God because doing so satisfies my need for cosmic security and meaning. It is just as appropriate for me to have faith, I feel, as it is for me to be with others or to eat.

This reasoning has appealed to countless people who have come to Christian faith. In reading and listening to accounts of how this has happened, one is struck by the fact that a prominent consideration is satisfaction of need. Consider one such journey. Allen was sixteen when he had the following experience.

ALLEN

I was at a church meeting and we sang the hymn, "Grace Greater Than All Our Sins." One of the verses says, "Dark is the stain we cannot hide, what can avail to wash it away? Look, there is flowing a crimson tide, brighter than snow you may be today." As I was going to bed that night, meditating on those words, for the first time in my life I had a sense of what it meant for Christ to suffer for my sin. I remember thinking, "I've never felt this before." It had never been experientially present to me—that complete cover offered to us in Christ's sacrifice for us.

I wept as I considered these things. I had never done that before. For the first time it was a matter of my sin, my stains.

In his twenties, after Allen left the nonliturgical tradition in which he grew up and started attending liturgical churches, he says,

> Somehow the most fundamental traditions of the church have become desperately important to me—little things in the liturgy: speaking the Lord's Prayer, reciting the Creeds, receiving the pastoral benediction and, supremely, communion. Somehow these things have assumed a kind of weight that they didn't have before. I really can't say how that happened. I find myself longing for the experience of communion. . . . I need to be near, I need to be as near as I can be to the body and the blood of the Lord. That is very much the center of my faith now.

The principal feature of Allen's teenaged experience is the need to deal with his own sin. He felt he could do that by taking in Christ's sacrifice for sin. The prominent feature of Allen's later experience is a longing for nearness. He believed that he could satisfy this longing by participating in church rituals, especially communion.

INSTANCES OF THE APPEAL TO NEED

The initial appeal of the argument is reinforced by the fact that numerous people have used need to try to convince others to acquire faith in God or to draw them to a deeper faith. Their doing so means they think that the satisfaction of need is a legitimate basis for coming to and continuing in faith. And it means they hope that some of those who listen to their entreaties will actually change as a result of the appeal. Let us look at some instances of such entreaties.

Jesus explicitly appeals to need in one of his most well-known invitations: "Come to me, all you that are weary and are carrying heavy burdens, and I will give you rest. Take my yoke upon you, and learn from me; for I am gentle and humble in heart, and you will find rest for your souls. For my yoke is easy, and my burden is light" (Mt 11:28-30). Here Jesus declares that he will give rest to those who are weary and are carrying heavy burdens if they come to him. Jesus assumes that people possess the need to be free from weariness and from carrying heavy burdens. "Coming to Jesus" no doubt involves having faith or trust in Jesus. Jesus declares that having this faith or trust satisfies the need: "I will give you rest." The inference, then, is that Jesus believes it is legitimate to have the trust. So there is something like the existential argument for believing in God in this invitation.

Jesus also appeals to need at the end of the Sermon on the Mount: "Everyone then who hears these words of mine and acts on them will be like a wise man who built his house on rock. . . . And everyone who hears these words of mine and does not act on them will be like a foolish man who built his house on sand" (Mt 7:24, 26). In this passage, Jesus makes the assumption that people possess a need for security and solidity, and he declares that obeying his teachings will bring that security. The inference is that Jesus believes obeying his teachings is legitimate because it satisfies the need.

Other places in the Bible mention need without appealing to it so explicitly. In Romans 8:1, Paul states, "There is therefore now no condemnation for those who are in Christ Jesus." In this declaration, Paul presupposes that people need to feel that they are not condemned. Those who are "in" Christ Jesus have this need satisfied. In Ephesians 2:4-5, Paul says, "But God, who is rich in mercy, . . . made us alive together with Christ." In this statement, Paul presupposes that people need to feel that they are "alive."

The Psalms contain numerous references to need. Here are two. "How long must I bear pain in my soul, and have sorrow in my heart all day long?" (Ps 13:2). Here the psalmist expresses a need to be free of pain in his soul and from sorrow all day long. "Wash me thoroughly from my iniquity, and cleanse me from my sin" (Ps 51:2). In this request to God, the psalmist presupposes a need to be free from his iniquity and sin. The assumption in both cases is that God can meet the needs that are expressed or presupposed.

Writers on Christian spirituality also appeal to need frequently. I shall mention two such appeals, chosen rather randomly. Thomas à Kempis, in his well-known *Imitation of Christ*, writes, "When Jesus is near, all is well and nothing seems difficult. When he is absent, all is hard. When Jesus does not speak within, all other comfort is empty, but if he says only a word, it brings great consolation."[2] Thomas is talking about the connection between Jesus being near and the satisfaction of need. When Jesus is near, he says, we experience comfort and consolation. When he is far or does not "speak within," we experience empty comfort and little consolation. In these statements, he is clearly presupposing that we need comfort and consolation, and that it is legitimate to let Jesus get near us so we may acquire them.

In her *The Christian's Secret of a Happy Life*, Hannah Whitehall Smith writes, "Many Christians, as I have said, love God's will in the abstract, but carry great burdens in connection with it. From this also there is deliverance in the wonderful life of faith. For in this way of life no burdens are carried, no anxieties felt. The Lord is our burden-bearer, and upon him we must lay off every care."[3] Smith explicitly presupposes that people want to be free from the overbearing burden of having to do God's will. The method by which people can become free of this burden, she says, is for "believers to *want* to do God's will as much as other people want to do their own will."[4] This wanting, she states, "is what God intended for us."[5] The life of faith, then, frees us from the burden of feeling that we have to do God's will even though we do not want to by giving us the desire to do God's will. Smith is assuming that appealing to the life of faith as a way of satisfying the believer's need to be free from a particular burden will be attractive to her readers.

These persons, from Jesus to Hannah Whitehall Smith, assume that an appeal to need is inviting to their listeners and readers. This fact reinforces my claim that the existential argument for believing in God is initially persuasive to many people.

---

[2]Thomas à Kempis, *Imitation of Christ*, trans. Leo Sherley-Price (London: Penguin Books, 1952), book 2, chap. 8, quoted in *Invitation to Christian Spirituality: An Ecumenical Anthology*, ed. John R. Tyson (New York: Oxford University Press, 1999), p. 199. Thomas lived 1380-1471 and was an Augustinian monk.

[3]Hannah Whitehall Smith, *The Christian's Secret of a Happy Life* (Old Tappan, N.J.: Fleming H. Revell, 1962), quoted in *Devotional Classics: Selected Readings for Individuals and Groups*, ed. Richard J. Foster and James Bryan Smith (New York: HarperSanFrancisco, 1990), p. 266. Hannah Whitehall Smith lived 1832-1911 and was a Quaker.

[4]Ibid., p. 265.

[5]Ibid.

EXISTENTIAL JUSTIFICATION

It is important to distinguish between the existential argument for believing in God and evidential arguments for believing in God. The existential argument does not give evidence for thinking that God exists. It says that faith in God is justified solely because it satisfies certain needs. In evidential justification for believing in God, one believes in God because of what one takes to be good evidence for doing so.

To get at the kind of justification involved in the existential argument, let us imagine that both of the premises in the existential argument are false, that is, that there are conditions in which there is no existential justification for believing in God. If one either did not have the needs mentioned in the first premise or did not find that faith in God satisfied the needs, then one would not be existentially justified in having faith in God. There would be nothing for the faith to do. Having it would be gratuitous—it would be had for nothing. But even if there were no existential justification for believing in God, there could well be evidential justification for doing so. The argument from design might show that there is a cosmic designer. The cosmological argument might show that there is an eternal and necessary being on which the physical universe depends for its existence. If these are good arguments, one would be justified in having faith in God, though it would be different from the faith that the existential argument would warrant. It would not be a faith designed to meet basic emotional and spiritual needs, but one designed to represent correctly the nature of reality. The faith based on satisfaction of need, however, is not aimed at representing correctly the nature of reality, but at meeting certain needs.

An analogy to eating can bring out the differences between the two types of justification. If one is hungry and if eating satisfies the hunger, then one is justified in eating. If one is not hungry, there would be no point in eating, and one would not be justified in doing so. (That's not quite true, of course. People eat for reasons other than to satisfy hunger.) The justification here is based solely on satisfying need. If, however, one were to argue that food is available because people get hungry, one would be giving evidence for believing something about the nature of reality. This argument claims something about what exists, whereas the former case is simply about whether an action justifiably assuages a need.

The existential argument for believing in God is like arguing that one is justified in eating if one is hungry—if one is "hungry" for God and if having faith in God satisfies this hunger, then one is justified in having faith in God. The argument is not meant to show that one is correct in believing that there is a God, just as in the hunger case the idea is not to prove that there is food nearby. Believing in God because doing so satisfies one's needs is different from believing that there is a God solely because of evidence.

THE EXISTENTIAL ARGUMENT DISTINGUISHED FROM EVIDENTIAL ARGUMENTS BASED ON NEED

Although there is a clear difference between existential and evidential justification, it is easy to confuse the existential argument for believing in God with an evidential argument based on need. To bring out further the difference between existential and evidential justification, several ways in which belief in God can be based on need evidentially are described below. These arguments use the presence of needs in humans to try to show that God exists or that Christianity is true.

God created people with needs. A first evidential argument says that we would not have certain needs unless there is a God who created us with them, because natural explanations of the presence of the needs fail. Consider the need to experience awe. One might try to give an evolutionary or Freudian explanation of wondering reverence tinged with fear, or one might try to give a neurological or psychological explanation of this emotion. But these explanations ultimately are unsatisfactory, the argument says. The evolutionary explanation does not work because wondering reverence has little or no survival value, as survival is understood in evolution. The Freudian explanation does not work because the source of wondering reverence cannot be traced to unconscious causes, let alone sexual ones. The neurological explanation may give a correct account of what goes on in one's brain when one feels the need to experience awe, but so also does a neurological explanation of how we see. And we would not infer from this latter fact that there is nothing outside us that we are seeing. The same point applies to a psychological explanation of the need to experience awe. So although neurological and psychological explanations for possessing the need to experience awe may be correct, they are not complete. The only explanation for the need to experience awe that is both correct and complete, the argument states, is that God made humans with the need. People have existential needs because God made them with these needs.

This evidential argument is like the existential argument for believing in God in that it purports to describe correctly basic emotional and spiritual needs. But the similarity ends there. The evidential argument tries to support the existence of God by showing that God's existence is needed to explain how people got those needs, whereas the existential argument tries to show that we can justifiably have faith in God solely because it satisfies the needs. The existence of various needs is used as evidence in the evidential argument, but not in the existential argument. Someone might be convinced that the existence of needs can be used as evidence for God's existence, but not be convinced that the satisfaction of needs by itself can be used to justify faith in God.

Christianity correctly describes human needs. A second evidential argument says that one reason for thinking that Christianity is true is that it correctly describes certain human needs. Christianity is based on the premise that people need cosmic security, unconditional love and forgiveness. When we look independently at what people need, we find that they do, indeed, have these needs. We can infer, the argument concludes, that Christianity is true or at least that an element of Christianity is true.

Blaise Pascal, in his attempt to convince people to embrace Christianity, used something like this argument: "Man's greatness and wretchedness are so evident that the true religion must necessarily teach us that there is in man some great principle of greatness and some great principle of wretchedness."[6] Christianity teaches that we have this dual nature, Pascal claimed. God made us good, but we have sinned, tarnishing the goodness but not eradicating it. And we can easily observe

[6]Blaise Pascal, *Pensées,* trans. A. J. Krailsheimer (New York: Penguin Books, 1995), #149 (p. 46).

this dual nature: "How novel, how monstrous, how chaotic, how para-
doxical, how prodigious! Judge of all things, feeble earthworm, reposi-
tory of truth, sink of doubt and error, glory and refuse of the universe!"[7]
So Christianity must be the true religion or at least a true religion, Pascal claimed, because observation supports one of its central claims.

Like the first evidential argument, this one uses the existence of
needs to try to support the truth of a claim, in this case, that Christianity is true. It does not say that we may have faith in God simply because
doing so satisfies these needs, as the existential argument does.

Predicting the satisfaction of needs. A third evidential argument says
that another reason for thinking that Christianity is true is that Christianity says that if people possess the right kind of faith, their basic
needs will be met. These needs can in fact be met, as can be observed.
We will, of course, have to exercise care in distinguishing their genuinely being met from their superficially being met. But when we do, we
find that they are genuinely being met. From this we can infer that the
people in whom they are being met have a faith that rightly represents
what actually exists, namely, God.

The existential argument for believing in God is like this evidential
one in asserting that faith in God, or specifically Christian faith, satisfies certain needs. The two differ in how this satisfaction is used. In the
evidential argument, the fact that the needs are satisfied is used to support the truth of Christianity. The existential argument, however, is
not aimed at supporting the truth of Christianity or theism, nor at
showing that the people whose needs are being met have a correct faith
(that is, one that rightly represents what is real). The aim of the existential argument is solely to show that one is justified in having faith. And
the justification here does not mean that one is warranted in believing
that Christianity or theism is true. It means only that one is warranted
in having a faith that satisfies the needs.

One might think that need or the satisfaction of need can be used as
evidence for believing in God, but not think that we are justified in
having faith in God just because it satisfies needs. What is needed, this

---

[7]Ibid., #131 (p. 34).

person would say, is evidence for the truth of God's existence or of Christianity, which the existential argument does not supply.

In general the difference between the existential and evidential arguments is that the existential argument says that we may legitimately believe in God because doing so satisfies certain needs, whereas the evidential ones say that God must exist or that Christianity must be true if we are to account for certain facts about needs—that we have them at all or that they can be satisfied. Although both kinds of arguments are need-based, they use needs in different ways, one as drawing people to faith and the other as evidence for the correctness of faith. A person who is convinced of an existential argument says, "I believe because I am satisfied when I do." A person who is convinced of an evidential argument says, "I believe because there is a good reason to do so."

SOME EXAMPLES

It will be helpful to give some examples of actual existential arguments and need-based evidential ones. Richard Swinburne, a British philosopher who is well known for his philosophical defense of theism, gives three nonfaith-related cases in which people believe solely on the basis of need:

- The mother who has to believe that her son is alive unless she is to go to pieces psychologically.

- The husband who has to believe that his wife is faithful if he is to avoid maltreating her.

- The lawyer who has to believe that his client is innocent if he is to make a good speech in his defence.[8]

In none of these cases do the individuals rely on evidence for their beliefs. The mother does not check with police departments for her wandering son. The husband does not hire a private detective to follow his wife's movements. The lawyer does not weigh the negative evidence against the positive evidence but goes only with the positive evidence.

---

[8]Richard Swinburne, *Faith and Reason*, 2nd ed. (Oxford: Clarendon, 2005), p. 77. Swinburne does not endorse the reasoning in the examples. He simply gives them as clear-cut cases that contrast with evidential reasoning.

The mother and the husband believe only to avoid grievous emotional consequences, and the lawyer only to perform well in court. These cases are like the following faith-related case:

- The person who has to believe in God if she is to avoid constant anguish about cosmic security, life beyond the grave and what a good life involves.

This person, too, does not rely on evidence for life beyond the grave. She does not examine philosophical or theological arguments. She believes only to avoid emotional distress. In each of these cases, there is something like the existential argument for believing in God: someone believes something not because they have evidence for its truth but because by doing so they satisfy certain needs.

A more extended instance of an existential argument comes from Ernest Becker, in his magisterial *The Denial of Death*. He begins by asserting, "of all things that move man, one of the principal ones is his terror of death."[9] To deal with this terror, we engage in what Becker calls "immortality projects."[10] These are activities we use to try to achieve immortality. Some people build monuments to themselves, others write books and still others try to acquire a wide reputation by being successful in some enterprise. Most immortality projects, however, are more subtle than these, Becker says. Sometimes we identify with a heroic person whom we think of as impervious to death and decay, so that we think we must be impervious too. Sometimes we deify someone with whom we have fallen in love—they are perfect, so our association with them makes us feel invulnerable to the hazards of imperfection. Often we participate in cultural practices, such as "commercial industrialism"[11] or the exercise of power,[12] that make us feel we are heroes, not just everyday ones, but cosmic ones who will not die. "Societies," Becker states, "are standardized systems of death denial; they give structure to the formulas for heroic transcendence."[13]

---

[9]Ernest Becker, *The Denial of Death* (New York: Free Press, 1973), p. 11.
[10]Ernest Becker, *Escape from Evil* (New York: Free Press, 1975), pp. 3, 63-65.
[11]Becker, *Denial of Death*, p. 271.
[12]Ibid., p. 152.
[13]Becker, *Escape from Evil*, pp. 153-54.

Becker's observation about these ways of denying death is, of course, that none of them work. The monuments decay, books are forgotten, reputations dissipate. The heroes and beloved persons with whom we identify and the cultural practices in which we participate all die. We are victims of our desperate desire for immortality. Becker spends a good deal of time in *The Denial of Death* and *Escape from Evil* explaining how we deceive ourselves into believing that we can escape death by these methods.

There is, however, Becker claims, a way in which we can satisfactorily believe that we will escape death. This is to identify with "something higher" than all of the unworkable ways of acquiring immortality.[14] He makes it plain that this something more is not susceptible to the ravages of death and decay. It is invisible,[15] an "absolute measure of power and value,"[16] a "transcendental support for one's life,"[17] "independent of living external rituals and customs,"[18] a "Higher Majesty" that dubs one a knight of faith.[19] It is, in fact, God. Becker's occasional references to God, the use of descriptive phrases that can apply only to God, and the fact that he has elsewhere identified himself as a Christian, make this conclusion clear.[20]

We can, then, interpret Becker as espousing an existential argument: We desperately desire immortality. The only satisfactory way to meet this desire is to believe in something that can guarantee our immortality. Identifying with heroes and participating in cultural practices that make us feel as if we are heroes do not guarantee immortality. Therefore, we are justified in believing in something beyond these heroes and practices—God, as God is the only entity that can guarantee immortality.[21]

---

[14]Becker, *Denial of Death*, p. 120.

[15]Ibid., pp. 258-59.

[16]Ibid., p. 195.

[17]Ibid., p. 200.

[18]Ibid.

[19]Ibid., p. 258.

[20]Becker identifies himself as a Christian in Harvey Bates, "Letters from Ernest," *Christian Century*, March 9, 1977, pp. 217-27, and as a theist in Sam Keen, "The Heroics of Everyday Life: A Theorist of Death Confronts His Own End," *Psychology Today* 7 (April 1974): 71-80.

[21]Becker did not explicitly cast either *The Denial of Death* or *Escape from Evil* as existential arguments for believing in God. But casting these books as existential arguments is true to what he says in them and illuminates their structure.

Another example of evidential arguments that are based on need comes from N. T. Wright, a New Testament scholar and another British writer. He writes in his popular defense of Christianity, *Simply Christian*, "The Christian story claims to be the true story about God and the world. As such, it offers itself as the explanation of the voice whose echo we hear in the search for justice, the quest for spirituality, the longing for relationship, the yearning for beauty."[22] In his book, Wright spends time describing these four voices. They turn out to be what I have called needs: we need justice, spirituality, relationships and beauty. The question is, where did we get these needs? Wright asserts in this passage that Christianity offers an explanation of how we got them. Simply put, it is that God gave them to us. To the extent that this explanation is plausible, Wright seems to be saying, Christianity is a true story about God and the world, in particular, a true story about human nature. Human nature is as it is, with its four basic needs, because God made it that way. We have here, then, a clear instance of an evidential argument that appeals to human needs. It seems closest to the first of the three evidential arguments I described above—the existence of the needs in humans is best explained by saying that God created us with them.

To be fair to Wright, he seems to view his argument more modestly than he states in the above quote. Immediately after it he adds, "None of these [four voices] by itself points directly to God—to any God, let alone the Christian God. At best, they wave their arms in a rather general direction, like someone in a cave who hears an echoing voice but has no idea where it's coming from."[23] With these words, he seems to take back what he just got through saying, namely, that the four voices, or needs, can be explained by appealing to the Christian God. Here he says only that the voices can be explained by something other than natural causes, but we don't know what that something is. If this is so, then his argument would not have as much force as he first seemed to claim. Which of these he really intended to say, however, does not mat-

---

[22]N. T. Wright, *Simply Christian: Why Christianity Makes Sense* (New York: HarperSanFrancisco, 2006), p. 55.
[23]Ibid.

ter for my present concern, as I merely want to point out a clear case of an evidential argument.

C. S. Lewis, in his well-known *Mere Christianity*, also uses a need-based evidential argument to support the truth of Christianity: "Creatures are not born with desires unless satisfaction of those desires exists. . . . If I find in myself a desire which no experience in this world can satisfy, the most probable explanation is that I was made for another world."[24] The tip-off that this is an evidential argument is that Lewis appeals to the idea of an explanation. Existential arguments contain nothing of an explanation in them, whereas evidential arguments do. The role of need in an existential argument is simply to move one to faith, whereas the role of need in an evidential argument is to provide a fact that needs explaining.

Lewis's argument is deceptively simple. If we were to reconstruct it in a step-by-step way, we would find a number of premises. Let us try sorting them out. His first statement is that if creatures are born with desires, then those desires must be satisfied. The desires Lewis pounces on are ones that cannot be satisfied "in this world," that is, before we die. The chapter in which this need-based evidential argument is contained deals with hope, especially the hope of heaven. We are born with a desire for heaven, Lewis states, or at least we find ourselves having it. But this desire cannot be satisfied by anything this side of the grave, as the invariable failure of our attempts to satisfy it shows. Since it must be satisfied, it will have to be satisfied after we die. And since it cannot be satisfied after we die unless there is a God who guarantees that it will be satisfied, there must be such a God. Moreover, this God will have instilled the desire for heaven in us at birth, or if not then, at least at some later point. This conclusion, Lewis says, is the most probable explanation of the fact that we have a desire that cannot be satisfied in this life.

Unfortunately, not all writers are as clear as Swinburne, Wright and Lewis when it comes to distinguishing existential from evidential arguments for believing in God. John Henry Newman, still another

---

[24]C. S. Lewis, *Mere Christianity* (New York: HarperCollins, 2001), pp. 136-37.

British writer (though from the nineteenth century) endorses the argument that "the Catholic religion is true . . . because it has never been to me anything but peace, joy, consolation and strength, all through my troubled life."[25] Is Newman saying that the Christian faith is true because it soothes his troubled life, or is he saying that it is legitimate to have Christian faith because it soothes his troubled life, apart from the question of whether it is true? He does not specify which reasoning he is using. Later, however, he presents a case that pretty clearly contains an existential argument. It is the case of a poor, dying factory girl described in Elizabeth Gaskell's novel *North and South*. The factory girl says:

> I think if this should be the end of all, and if all I have been born for is just to work my heart and life away, and to sicken in this dree place, with those mill-stones in my ears for ever, until I could scream out for them to stop and let me have a little piece of quiet, and with the fluff filling my lungs, until I thirst to death for one long deep breath of the clear air, and my mother gone, and I never able to tell her again how I loved her, and of all my troubles,—I think, if this life is the end, and that there is no God to wipe away all tears from all eyes, I could go mad![26]

The poor factory girl would go mad if she did not believe that there is life beyond the grave, a life in which God comforts her sorrow, gives her rest and frees her from the misery she feels. She does not appear to have any thought of an evidential argument in mind, one in which she believes that God must exist as explanation of her need to be free from inner torment. Her reasoning, if that is what it can be called, seems to be something like this:

1. I badly need not to be mad.

2. I can avoid going mad by believing that God will free me from all my troubles after I die.

3. Therefore, I am justified in believing that God will free me from all my troubles after I die.

[25]John Henry Newman, *An Essay in Aid of a Grammar of Assent*, ed. with introduction and notes by I. T. Ker (Oxford: Oxford University Press, 1985), p. 139.
[26]Elizabeth Gaskell, *North and South*, quoted in Newman, *Grammar of Assent*, p. 202.

She seems to be saying, in other words, that she believes God will free her from her troubles because she needs to believe it. Newman approves of the factory girl's reasoning. So although it is not certain whether he intended to put forward an existential argument in the earlier passage, it is fairly certain here.

The factory girl's reasoning is exactly the sort of reasoning that appears to take place in many people's minds when they come to Christian faith. They cannot live with a constant sense of guilt, so they embrace God's forgiveness. They must have meaning in their lives, one involving something more than trivial aims, so they adopt the aim of pleasing God in what they do.

Though this existential reasoning seems to be used by many ordinary people, not many defenders of the Christian faith have used it. One significant exception is Blaise Pascal, a seventeenth-century mathematician and Christian apologist. In his classic *Pensées* he uses both evidential arguments and what I interpret as existential ones to support his claim that the Christian faith should be embraced. Dealing with what Pascal says will highlight the issues that are involved in sorting out the difference between existential and evidential arguments.

PASCAL

Pascal's aim in *Pensées* is to persuade people to become Christians. To do this he employs what appear to be two strategies. First he gives reasons for thinking that Christianity is true. He calls these reasons "proofs." Among the proofs that he appeals to are miracles, prophecies in the Old Testament, the perpetuity of the Jewish religion, the testimony of the apostles and the divinity of Jesus.[27] Consider the second of these:

> If a single man had written a book foretelling the time and manner of Jesus's coming and Jesus had come in conformity with these prophecies, this would carry infinite weight. But there is much more here. There is a succession of men over a period of 4,000 years, coming consistently and invariably one after the other, to foretell the same coming.[28]

---

[27]For a list of these proofs see Pascal, *Pensées*, #482 (p. 153).
[28]Ibid., #332 (p. 101).

In this passage and others like it, Pascal is attempting to show that the information contained in the Old Testament prophecies about Jesus was given to the prophets by God. It is not reasonable to suppose that the same information coming from so many different sources at so many different times could simply have been guessed at or made up. It must have had a divine origin, Pascal concludes. The other reasons that Pascal gives for believing that Christianity is true—his "proofs"—all have the same evidential form: reasons purporting to show that statements essential to Christianity are true.

Pascal's second strategy for persuading people to become Christians, his existential apologetics, consists of showing that having Christian faith satisfies deep human needs. In this strategy, Pascal is not producing evidence for the truth of Christianity. He is not setting up an argument with the conclusion that some element of Christianity is true. He is, rather, describing human needs and claiming that having Christian faith satisfies these needs. Let us look at several of Pascal's statements that can be interpreted as claiming this, beginning with the well-known passage about the infinite abyss in humans. He writes,

> What else does this craving, and this helplessness, proclaim but that there was once in man a true happiness, of which all that now remains is the empty print and trace? This he tries in vain to fill with everything around him, seeking in things that are not there the help he cannot find in those that are, though none can help, since this infinite abyss can be filled only with an infinite and immutable object; in other words by God himself.[29]

The infinite abyss, Pascal tells us, is a craving for true happiness. Humans once had true happiness, but now have only the craving for it. The craving has remained despite the fall of Adam and Eve (which shows that the fall did not entirely obliterate all good in humans, as the craving for what is good is itself good). People try to satisfy the craving by means of natural objects and activities. But these do not work. Only God can satisfy it. The craving is like a distinctively shaped space into which only God can fit. Humans try to put other objects into the space,

---

[29]Ibid., #148 (p. 45).

but none actually can go in. C. S. Lewis calls this distinctive space a hollow into which only God can fit.[30]

This passage might be thought to contain an evidential argument. If it did, Pascal would be arguing that God must exist because otherwise we humans could not satisfy the craving we have for God. Only God's actual existence could fill the infinite abyss in us. To get to the conclusion that God exists, Pascal would also have to say that the abyss is actually filled, for otherwise God might not exist even if the only thing that could fill the abyss is God. Human life would then be a useless passion, as Jean Paul Sartre put it. With the additional assertion, Pascal's argument, interpreted evidentially, would go like this:

1. Humans have an indefinite and intense craving for true happiness.

2. Only God can satisfy this craving.

3. The craving can be satisfied.

4. Therefore, God exists.

This interpretation of the infinite abyss passage fits the words that Pascal uses: "this infinite abyss can be filled only with an infinite and immutable object; in other words by God himself."[31] Here Pascal is talking about God and not just about faith in God. So it looks as if he is arguing that it is reasonable to believe that God exists because we crave to know God and because the craving can be satisfied.

One can also interpret the infinite abyss passage existentially. In this interpretation it is not that God satisfies the craving for God, but that faith in God satisfies the craving, just as it is not food that satisfies hunger, but that eating food does. Interpreted existentially, Pascal's argument would look like this:

1. Humans have an indefinite and intense craving for true happiness.

2. Only faith in God satisfies this craving.

---

[30]C. S. Lewis, *The Problem of Pain* (New York: HarperCollins, 2001), p. 152. "Your soul has a curious shape because it is a hollow made to fit a particular swelling in the infinite contours of the divine substance." This passage is the source of the often-stated remark that Lewis asserted that humans have a "God-shaped vacuum" in them.

[31]Pascal, *Pensées*, #148 (p. 45).

3. If only faith in God satisfies this craving, then we are justified in having it.

4. Therefore, we are justified in having faith in God.

The difference between this argument and the evidential one is that the conclusion in the evidential one states that an important claim in Christianity is true, whereas the conclusion in this one states that having faith in God is "justified"—not in the sense that it is true or in the sense that it mirrors reality, but in the sense that it is legitimate to have the faith. It is legitimate because it brings about the satisfaction of the indefinite and intense craving mentioned in the first premise.

Although the infinite abyss passage might be thought of as an evidential argument, it is, I believe, more plausibly interpreted as an existential one. Though Pascal himself did not make it clear which one he was espousing, he gives hints that point toward an existential interpretation. One is that immediately subsequent to the list of evidential arguments that Pascal uses in the *Pensées,* which include his arguments based on miracles, prophecies and the perpetuity of the Jewish religion, he appeals to the inclination of the heart to embrace God: "Without any doubt after this, considering the nature of life and of this religion, we ought not to resist the inclination to follow it if our hearts are so inclined."[32] Pascal seems to be making the distinction here between evidence that shows that a religion is true and inclination to follow the religion. This distinction is precisely the one I have been drawing between evidential arguments and existential ones. The former presents reasons for thinking that belief in God is true, whereas the latter argues that if believing in God satisfies our inclination to believe, we may properly do so.

In addition, this distinction between evidence and inclination seems to be what Pascal had in mind, at least some of the time, when he distinguished between reason and the heart. He writes,

- The heart has its reasons of which reason knows nothing: we know this in countless ways.[33]

- It is the heart which perceives God and not the reason. That is what

---

[32]Pascal, *Pensées,* #482 (p. 153).
[33]Ibid., #423 (p. 127).

faith is: God perceived by the heart, not by the reason.[34]

In these famous quotes, Pascal is saying that there is a sharp differ-ence between the way in which reason knows God and the way in which the heart knows God. The heart knows God by perceiving God. Pascal does not say how reason knows God, but he clearly means that it does not do so by perceiving. If we think of reason as a reason-producing faculty, as Pascal does when he puts forward his evidential arguments for believing in God, then we can interpret Pascal as saying that reason knows God by producing reasons for God's existence or for thinking that God has a certain nature. In other words, reason pro-duces arguments about God, and believing the conclusions of these arguments is what constitutes knowing God through reason.

The heart, however, knows God directly, through perception, not through arguments. And this perception is a kind of reason: "The heart has its reasons." It is not reason in the customary sense of reason—"of which reason knows nothing"—that is, the kind of reason that counts as evidence for the truth of another claim. It is, I suggest, a "reason" based on inclination, or the satisfaction of a need. It is "reasonable" to know God directly, through perception or intuition, if doing so satis-fies our inclination to know God. When we apply the idea of inclina-tion being a "reason" for believing in God to the infinite abyss passage, we get this reconstruction:

> The heart has an empty place in it. This place is like an abyss because it is so large—a gaping hole that we desperately desire to be filled. We want to know God or love God or be connected to God in some way. And when we actually are connected to God, or at least believe that we are, the gaping hole is filled. This, we think, is as good a "reason" to believe in God as any. A need has been satisfied, an inclination appeased.

Other passages in Pascal's *Pensées* seem to contain inclination arguments like this reconstruction of the infinite abyss passage. Here are two:

> No one is so happy as a true Christian, or so reasonable, virtuous, and lovable.[35]

---

[34]Ibid., #424 (p. 127).
[35]Ibid., #357 (p. 106).

The Christian religion alone has been able to cure these twin vices ["pride or sloth, the twin sources of all vice"], not by using one to expel the other according to worldly wisdom, but by expelling both through the simplicity of the Gospel.[36]

Though these passages, like the infinite abyss passage, might be construed as containing evidential arguments, they are better construed as containing existential arguments. Acquiring Christian faith makes us happier than otherwise, so we are justified in acquiring it. And becoming a Christian cures us of pride and sloth, so it is fitting that we become one. Of course, the assumptions here are that we want to be happy and that we want to be cured of pride and sloth. With these assumptions, which are reasonable, and with the assertion that being a Christian fulfills these wants, we can legitimately embrace Christian faith, Pascal says. We are justified in letting Christian faith satisfy our desires.

A short way of distinguishing between the evidential and existential arguments that Pascal uses is to say that in the former we ought to believe because there are good reasons for thinking our beliefs are true, whereas in the latter we may believe because we need to, or more strongly, that we ought to believe because doing so is the only way of satisfying our needs.

THE POINT OF THE DISTINCTION

Is there a point to making the distinction between the two kinds of arguments besides simply clarifying the difference between the two? Is there any interest in the distinction for everyday persons as opposed to professional philosophers? I believe there is.

In the first place, there is the question of how best faith can be secured—how, that is, it can be acquired and made stable and firm. If my thesis in this book is right, namely, that the ideal way to secure one's faith is through both need and reason, then one must know what both of these ways are. The distinction between the two ways is not just theoretical, but has real-life import.

In addition, there is the question of how people of faith can defend

---

[36]Ibid., #208 (p. 68).

their faith. Those who do not have faith sometimes dismiss the legitimacy of faith with the remark, "Faith is just a product of emotions." The idea behind this dismissal is that believing something just because one feels a need to believe it does not make it true. Perhaps, too, the critic believes that the emotions that produce faith are signs of weakness and not of strength of character. People of faith, then, must do two things to respond to this dismissal of faith. They must first be clear about whether their faith actually is based on emotions. If it is, then, second, they must defend that basis. And doing this involves doing something different from defending faith on the grounds that the evidence for it is good. Using the satisfaction of need to bring about faith is different from using need as evidence for the truth of faith. Defending the legitimacy of the former involves one kind of "reasoning," and defending the legitimacy of the latter involves a different kind of reasoning. If these two types of reasoning are not clearly distinguished, then the defense of one's faith will miss the mark.

NEED AND REASON

The initial plausibility of existential arguments comes from the fact that we are creatures with needs. We need to believe that our children are safe, our spouses faithful and our clients innocent. And we need to feel awe, cosmic security, inner peace and hope for a better future. For some of us, these needs are insistent, and we find ourselves assuaging them almost automatically, that is, without conscious choice. Doing so is instinctual, like eating when we are hungry.

When we satisfy our needs, we view ourselves as doing something reasonable. The mother who avoids falling to pieces by believing that her son is alive thinks of herself as being reasonable, or she would think of herself as being reasonable if she reflected on what she is thinking. She is preserving her sanity. Having the belief keeps her stable and free from debilitating worry. In the same way, those who have faith in God because it keeps them free from debilitating anxiety think of their faith as being reasonable. It preserves them from emotional distress.

We can call the reasonableness in these cases *need reasonableness* or *need rationality*. In need rationality, those who satisfy their needs by believing certain things are being sensible and wise. They are taking care of themselves. Need rationality consists of successfully satisfying needs.

Need rationality differs from what William James, an early twentieth-century American philosopher, called "merely logical" rationality.[37] This kind of rationality is purely intellectual. The satisfaction of needs is irrelevant to being rational in this sense (unless one is putting forward an evidential argument based on the satisfaction of needs). Indeed, the satisfaction of needs is sometimes a hindrance to being rational in this sense. This is because merely logical rationality consists of being objective and impartial about matters of truth. Because needs are not objective or impartial, they can obstruct our believing what is true. And believing what is true is the aim of merely logical rationality.

Like need rationality, merely logical rationality is based on a fact about human nature, namely, that we are creatures of reason. Because of this fact, we want our beliefs to be true, and we want the evidence for them to be good. We do not necessarily want evidence for all our beliefs, as acquiring it would require more time and energy than we have, but we do want evidence for certain important beliefs. We also want our beliefs to be objective, that is, not influenced by extraneous needs and emotions.

The question of this book can be cast in this way: to what extent should need rationality be involved in acquiring and maintaining faith? Partisans of logical rationality will answer this question with, "None at all. We need to know that our faith is correct, and if we let our needs influence our faith, we could not be sure of that." To the partisans of logical rationality, we would be irrational if we let our needs influence our faith. For them, only evidential arguments are pertinent to the justification of faith.

Partisans of need rationality can answer the question in two ways. They can say, "It is legitimate for our needs to generate faith because it is reasonable for us to satisfy needs and because faith satisfies certain

---

[37]William James, "The Sentiment of Rationality," in *The Writings of William James*, ed. John J. McDermott (New York: Modern Library, 1968), p. 325.

needs. We would be irrational not to let need propel us to faith." For those who answer in this way, existential arguments are sufficient to generate faith. Partisans of need rationality can also answer the question in a second way by saying, "We should base faith on both need and reason, because we are creatures of both need and reason. We would be irrational not to let both features of our nature generate faith." For those who answer in this second way, both existential and evidential arguments are needed to support faith. For them, being rational includes both need rationality and logical rationality.

William James adopted this broader conception of being rational: "Of two conceptions equally fit to satisfy the logical demand, that one which awakens the active impulse, or satisfies other aesthetic demands better than the other, will be accounted the more rational conception, and will deservedly prevail."[38] James is saying that the logical conception of being rational is too narrow. It illegitimately neglects our non-logical nature. What must be added to the logical demand—but not substituted for it—is satisfaction of nonlogical demands.

This book defends such a broader conception of rationality. The ideal way to acquire and maintain faith is to listen to both our needs and reason. We can acquire faith on evidential arguments alone or on existential arguments alone, because people have actually done so, but to do either is not as secure as acquiring it in both ways. What follows will demonstrate how need rationality can be supplemented with logical rationality. The existential argument for believing in God may be initially plausible, but it must be supplemented with reason for it to be finally credible.

Said another way, though the existential argument for believing in God is initially persuasive to many people, it is also initially unpersuasive to many people. The four objections considered in chapters four through seven are also initially persuasive. In fact, some people who find the existential argument persuasive no doubt ask themselves one or more of the questions on which the objections are based: Can satisfaction of need really establish truth? Would not one also be justified in

---

[38] Ibid., p. 325.

believing in a cosmic tyrant? Do not lots of people feel no need for God? And do not lots of people satisfy the needs mentioned in the existential argument without faith in God? These are obvious questions, and they create the puzzle that this book discusses. I turn now to the first of them.

4

OBJECTION ONE

Pᴇʀʜᴀᴘꜱ ᴛʜᴇ ꜰɪʀꜱᴛ ǫᴜᴇꜱᴛɪᴏɴ ᴛʜᴀᴛ ᴏᴄᴄᴜʀꜱ to one who encounters the existential argument for believing in God is, can't our needs be satisfied by believing in something that does not actually exist? This question prompts the objection that basing belief in God solely on satisfaction of need is illegitimate, because God might not exist even though believing in God satisfies our needs for cosmic security and life beyond the grave. We can call this objection the Invisible George Objection, because it says that the existential argument for believing in God is like arguing that it is legitimate to believe that Invisible George accompanies us wherever we go since doing so satisfies our need to feel secure. So, says the objection, the existential argument for believing in God is analogous to the following fallacious argument.

1. We need to feel secure.

2. Believing that Invisible George accompanies us wherever we go satisfies this need.

3. Therefore, we are justified in believing that Invisible George accompanies us wherever we go.

The obvious problem with this argument, the objection says, is that there might be no invisible person accompanying us wherever we go, even though believing there is satisfies our need to feel secure. Similarly, it might be that there is no God even though believing that there is satisfies our need for cosmic security.

But, we must ask, what is wrong with believing that Invisible George protects us? If believing this gives us serenity and assuages our anxiety, then we would be justified in believing it simply because it works. It would not matter that George does not exist so long as the believing was efficacious. A similar argument holds for the factory girl in Elizabeth Gaskell's novel or, to take another case, a soldier at war who has not heard from her fiancé in some time. Why should the soldier not believe that her beloved still loves her if doing so keeps her from falling to pieces, or the factory girl not trust that God will make things right after she dies to keep herself from incapacitating anguish now? If having faith in God satisfies certain needs, then why can't we have the faith even if God does not exist?

The answer, according to the Invisible George Objection, is that we want our beliefs not only to satisfy our needs but also to be true, and merely satisfying needs does not guarantee truth. Because of this, we should not let such satisfaction be a cause of belief. The soldier should not believe that her fiancé still loves her simply because doing so would keep her from incapacitating anguish. The factory girl should not believe that there is a God who will give her peace after she dies simply because believing this would cause her to be free from inner torment. In each case, the troubled person wants the belief that calms her to be true, but the fact that the belief calms her does not show it to be true.

This point is surely right. It is not enough that our beliefs satisfy our needs. They must be true as well or we would regard them as deficient. So the Invisible George Objection is right. A purely existential justification of having faith in God is illegitimate. The existential argument for believing in God is defective.

ADDING REASON TO NEED

But things are not so simple as merely agreeing with the objection and then dismissing the existential argument, which is the customary response. Need has been such a driving force for believing in God that we should look for some way to legitimize that force. The way to do so, I believe, is to add the use of reason to need. In this chapter, I shall describe three ways in which this can be done, illustrating with an analogy to hunger.

Let us construct an argument for eating that is analogous to the existential argument for believing in God. It might go something like this:

1. Humans get hungry.

2. Eating food assuages hunger.

3. Therefore, eating food is justified.

We normally take this argument, or more accurately, the instinctive process that this argument represents, to justify eating. We are hungry, so we eat. Now suppose a critic says, "Just because people are hungry doesn't mean that food exists. It might be that people are hungry and that there is no food." This response is like the Invisible George Objection. And it is clearly right. But it is not the whole story. For someone who uses this hunger argument is presupposing that there is food. They are not using the argument to establish the existence of food but to justify eating it given that it already is known to exist. So the critic's response, though right, is irrelevant.

Now imagine that someone is hungry, but for some psychological reason is not attracted to eating. What could we do to get them to eat? Two things: the first would be to unpack the first premise, namely, to describe their hunger pangs, and the second would be to unpack the second premise, namely, to explain how eating alleviates the hunger and pleases one's appetite for taste and smell. Although doing these still might not prompt the person to eat because of the psychological issue, it would at least attract them to eating to some degree. The existential argument for believing in God has a similar function. A description of emotional and spiritual needs plus an account of how faith in God satisfies these needs can draw one to faith in God as much as smell draws one to food. The assumption in each case is that the object of our attraction exists—food in the eating argument and God in the faith argument. The existential argument for believing in God can thus be employed as a need argument with a cognitive assumption. In this way, though it succumbs to the Invisible George Objection, it still can be used. Its use would be to draw to faith in God people who already believe that God exists.

People who are drawn to faith in God by satisfaction of need often actually do presuppose that God exists. Consider Allen again, whose faith was spurred by the need to feel forgiven. It wasn't that this need brought about a belief that God exists or that Christianity is true. He already had those beliefs. Of his intense evening experience, he said, "I never doubted the Christian story, but I certainly felt it for the first time then." So it may be that both need and reason are involved when people come to faith. That, at any rate, is what seems to be shown by the accounts I have included in this book.

This, then, is the first way in which reason can be added to need—by believing that God exists. And this can be done in a fideist way or an evidentialist way. In the fideist way, no evidence for believing that God exists is present, and in the evidentialist way, evidence for believing that God exists is present. Fideism is the view that one does not need evidence to be warranted in believing in God, and evidentialism is the view that one does need evidence to be warranted in believing in God. I am not going to decide this issue here, as that is beyond the scope of this book. It is sufficient to note that both views involve reason—fideism because it adds something conceptual to need, namely, a belief in God, and evidentialism because it adds evidence to need, namely, reasons for believing in God. (The evidentialist, of course, would not admit the legitimacy of the fideist way of supplementing the existential argument for believing in God, but that is beside the point.) The satisfaction of need can be used to draw us to faith in God if it is supplemented with reason in some way, whether this way involves the unsupported belief that God exists or evidence supporting this belief.

USING NEED EXISTENTIALLY AND EVIDENTIALLY

The second way in which reason can be added to need is a special case of supplementing need with evidence—by using need both existentially and evidentially. The belief that God exists can be based on one of the need-based evidential arguments for believing in God that I described in the last chapter. If so, need would be used as evidence for thinking that there is a God and existentially for drawing one to faith in God. Here is how it might work: One wonders how humans can have so many of the needs listed in chapter two without there being a God who has given humans those needs. One feels some of those needs and then imagines how faith in God would satisfy those needs. Finally, one takes on faith in God.

Consider hunger again. Let us imagine a scenario in which an adult human is created whole, without being born. She is placed in a meadow, and her first awareness is of wildflowers spread out in all directions. She wanders among them, noting their colors and shapes. Soon she becomes hungry. She wonders what the increasing discomfort in her stomach is due to. If it gets too painful, she thinks, she will no longer be able to wander among the flowers. She likes them and wants to keep drifting among them, and because of this she thinks that perhaps the reason she was put into the meadow is to keep on enjoying the flowers. So, she concludes, there must be something that will alleviate her stomach pain so that she can keep doing that. It will be something as pleasant as the flowers, she thinks, something she will enjoy and delight in. She heads toward the edge of the meadow where she finds a variety of fruits growing on trees and shrubs, which, she discovers, eliminate her pain when she eats them and provide as much enjoyment as do the flowers.

In this fanciful scenario, Eve, if I may name her that, used need both evidentially and existentially. She reasoned to the conclusion that food must exist, and she was spurred to eat on the basis of need. Her evidential reasoning assumed that there is a reason for her continued presence in the meadow, and her existential reasoning assumed that eating provides enjoyment. If she had reasoned just existentially, we would think that she would be believing that there is food simply because she wanted it, and we would rightly regard this as fallacious, committing the Invisible George Fallacy. But not so if it were made against the evidential reasoning she employs. If the evidential reasoning is fallacious, it is not for the same reason that the existential reasoning is.

Now consider similar reasoning by the factory girl. It is possible that

she is using need just existentially: "I think, if this life is the end, and that
there is no God to wipe away all tears from all eyes, I could go mad!" But
suppose for a moment that she is doubtful about God. She has undergone
so much misfortune and grief that she wonders whether there really is a
God who cares for her. She gets to thinking, though: "Why do I have a
need to be free from worry and woe? Why do I want to live after I die in
a place where it will be quiet and where no one will hassle me? Maybe
God put this desire for a better place into me because God wanted me to
believe in this better place. I certainly do need to believe in a better place,
for I have had more than my share of trials and tribulation."

In this scenario, the factory girl, like Eve, is reasoning both evidentially and existentially. She comes to believe that God put the need for
a better place into her heart. In this, she is using need evidentially. She
also badly wants to believe in a better place, for she imagines herself
going mad if she does not. In this, she is using need existentially. If she
were to use need just existentially, we would respond as we did to Eve—
we cannot rightly believe in something just because we want to or think
we need to. But we could not respond in this way to her evidential use
of need.

What these scenarios show is that there is a place for the existential
argument for believing in God if it is combined with an evidential argument based on need. The Invisible George Objection does not have
force against this combined reasoning, because this reasoning is not
based simply on satisfaction of need.

COMBINED REASONING

Let us look more closely at how this combined reasoning would go.
Consider again the needs described in chapter two: for awe, cosmic
security, meaning, love and others. Several facts about these needs are
conspicuous. The first is that there are quite a few of them. This fact is
significant because objections to need-based arguments almost always
mention only one need. The question these objections pose is, could we
not feel a need for meaning even though there is no God to give meaning? However, this rhetorical question makes sense partly because only
one need is at stake. But if more than a dozen needs are at stake, the

question loses most of its force. It becomes, could we not feel a need for meaning, cosmic security, love, life beyond the grave, and an expansive life even though there is no God to give us these needs? The answer to this question is, yes, that is possible, but it would be a very odd fact about human nature if it had all of these needs and there were no God. That is, this is the answer that the evidential need-based argument would give. It says that the presence of so many needs cries out for an explanation, and the best explanation is that there is a God who has given humans the needs.

This is the best explanation, the evidential argument continues, because of three more facts about the needs. One is that they are all connected to God in some way, some more obviously so than others. Another is that they are connected to each other; they are not simply isolated, stand-alone needs. Still another is that everyone or nearly everyone has felt at least some of the needs at some point in their lives, and many people have felt most of them or even all of them.

When we combine this evidential reasoning with the existential argument for believing in God, we get the following:

1. We need to feel awe and cosmic security. We need to know that we will live beyond the grave in a state that is free from the defects of this life, a state that is full of goodness and justice. We need a more expansive life, one in which we love and are loved. We need meaning, and we need to know that we are forgiven for going astray.

2. The best explanation for the presence of these needs in humans is that there is a God who has put them into humans.

3. Faith in God satisfies these needs.

4. Therefore, we are justified in believing there is a God in whom we can have faith.

This argument is not simply an existential one, because it says that there is evidence for believing that there is a God who has given us needs. Nor is it simply an evidential argument, for it says that we are justified in having faith in God because doing so satisfies our needs. The faith that is justified existentially is not blind, as the Invisible George Objection claims, because it is conjoined with evidential reasoning.

Something like this combined argument may be what some people have in mind when they appeal to need as a basis for believing in God or Christianity. Here is an example, again from William James: "In what did the emancipating message of primitive Christianity consist but in the announcement that God recognizes those weak and tender impulses which paganism had so rudely overlooked?"[1] One of these weak and tender impulses, James says, is repentance: "Christianity took it, and made it the one power within us which appealed straight to the heart of God."[2] The argument that James attributes to primitive Christianity looks as if it appeals both to reason and the heart. It is an appeal to reason because it says that Christianity is true and paganism false on the grounds that Christianity's conception of human nature is more accurate than paganism's. Paganism overlooks the need to repent. So it has less evidence in its favor than Christianity has. In addition, the argument appeals to the human heart because by repentance one could go straight to the heart of God. James assumes here that humans dearly want to please God. So the need for repentance had both an evidential and an existential function in primitive Christianity, according to James, if my reconstruction of his comments is right.

NEED AS A TRIGGERING CONDITION

There is a third way reason can be involved in coming to believe in God via need. It might be that need is acting not as an element in an evidential argument, but as a triggering condition for belief. A triggering condition is an event or state that produces a belief without going through an inferential process. The belief is caused by the event; one does not construct an argument for the belief. A good example illustrating the difference between a triggering condition and an inferential process is the use of ordered complexity in coming to believe in God. The argument from design for believing in God says that the universe must have a maker because the ordered complexity in it requires a maker. Here,

---

[1]William James, "The Sentiment of Rationality," in *The Writings of William James,* ed. John J. McDermott (New York: Modern Library, 1968), p. 331.
[2]Ibid.

complexity, or the belief in complexity, operates as part of a reasoning process, short though it may be. If, however, the complexity (or the belief in complexity) were acting as a triggering condition, it would simply cause the belief in a cosmic designer without going through the reasoning process. The belief in a cosmic designer would be evoked by the complexity immediately without the intervening premise that complexity requires a designer. Upon encountering an instance of complexity, such as the way in which atoms and molecules are arranged or the fine tuning in the initial explosion of the universe, one simply comes to believe that it has a designer. It would be as if Eve were caused to believe that there is food because of her hunger instead of using her hunger to reason to the existence of food. In the terminology of Alvin Plantinga, the belief resulting from a triggering condition would be basic, because it does not rest on reasons. It has no foundation in argumentation, though it does have a cause. The cause, however, does not act as an argument does, namely, to convince via evidence.[3]

Now it may be that some people who are drawn to faith in God by the existential argument have obtained their belief that God exists via a triggering condition, such as from complexity in nature. They may simply find themselves having the belief that there is a God as a result of being confronted with an instance of intricate or majestic order, and then may conjoin this belief with the existential argument, which would cause them to embrace God emotionally as well as cognitively. Or it may be that their belief in God is triggered by the recognition of one of their own needs, such as the need to be loved. Consider a scenario in which someone is reflecting on the lack of love she has received from her parents. She laments this lack, and perhaps is somewhat angry at it as well. These feelings provoke in her an awareness of a strong need to be loved, a need which has not hitherto been met. And this in turn evokes in her the belief that there is a God who loves in the way she needs to be loved. Or consider a scenario in which someone is dismayed

---

[3]Alvin Plantinga, "Reason and Belief in God," in *Faith and Rationality: Reason and Belief in God,* ed. Alvin Plantinga and Nicholas Wolterstorff (Notre Dame, Ind.: University of Notre Dame Press, 1983), pp. 16-93, especially pp. 63-68, 78-82. Plantinga calls the belief in God that results from a triggering condition a "deliverance of reason."

at the appalling and horrific evil among humans. He finds himself longing for a state in which everyone treats everyone else with happy kindness and in which justice prevails. Both his dismay and his longing cause him to believe that there is a God who will bring about such a state. In neither of these scenarios is there an evidential argument. There is simply an awareness of a need and the resulting belief in God. If, then, we add the triggering condition to the existential argument, need would function as a cause of belief, and the desirability of having a need satisfied would draw one to belief. The use of need in both these ways would coalesce into one instinctive process.

It may be difficult to say in a given case whether need is operating evidentially or as a triggering condition. That should not prevent us from saying, however, that an existential appeal to need can be conjoined with a cognitive appeal to need via either an evidential argument or a triggering condition so as to meet the Invisible George Objection.

Although the existential argument for believing in God succumbs to the Invisible George Objection, these three ways in which reason can be added to need restore the usefulness of the existential argument: (1) assuming that God exists or that Christianity is true, (2) combining the existential argument with an evidential argument for God's existence or Christianity's truth, such as a need-based evidential argument, or (3) combining the existential argument with belief in God that has been triggered by some event, such as the recognition of one's need for God. Perhaps I should say, "especially when it is combined with a need-based evidential argument," and "especially when it is combined with belief in God that has been triggered by need," since in these cases need is used not only existentially but also as evidence or as a triggering condition, an approach that seems to have had a strong appeal to many believers.

THE IRRELEVANCY OBJECTION

But now a new objection arises, one the reader may have had in mind for some pages. If the existential argument is supplemented with an evidential one or accompanied by a belief in God that has been triggered by some event, then has not the existential argument become irrelevant? For if one believes in God via an evidential argument, no other argument is needed to become convinced. One would already be convinced. Richard Swinburne put it this way: "If such an inquiry [a rational one] concludes that it is likely that there is a God, then the non-rational reasons for cultivating belief that there is a God are irrelevant, for we would already believe."[4] What, in other words, is the point of adopting an existential argument for believing in God if an evidential argument justifies such believing or a triggering condition produces it?

BELIEFS THAT ARE CONNECTED TO NEED

The answer is that there is a difference between beliefs that have little or no connection to human needs and beliefs that have a great deal of connection to human needs. Those that have little or no connection require only evidential reasoning to make them convincing, but those that have a great deal of connection require both evidential and existential reasoning to make them convincing (unless fideism is true, in which case evidential reasoning is not required).

An example of a belief that has little or no connection to human need is the claim that light bends as it travels past large astronomical objects. Einstein's general theory of relativity predicted this in 1915, but the claim was not confirmed until 1919, when astronomers observed the path of a distant star that had just passed from behind the sun during an eclipse of the sun. The observed location of the star differed from the location where astronomers had calculated the star would appear had light from the star not bent as it passed the sun. And the observed location was what the complicated mathematical formulae of the theory of relativity predicted, given that light bends as it passes large astronomical objects, such as the sun. In this case, typical of many cases in physics, astronomy and chemistry, human need played very little role. Although the general need to discover the truth about the universe lay behind the claim, none of the specific needs mentioned in the existential argument for believing in God (nor other psychological needs) were involved in convincing anyone that the claim was true.

One example of a belief that has a great deal of connection to human

---

[4]Richard Swinburne, *Faith and Reason*, 2nd ed. (Oxford: Clarendon, 2005), p. 132.

need is the claim that an emotional hermit would have a richer life with love in it. An emotional hermit is one who has shut himself off from feeling love. He distances himself from those who want to display affection toward him, and he rarely displays affection toward anyone. Though he walks and talks among numerous acquaintances, he is a hermit. It is easy for those who are not emotional hermits to see that emotional hermits would have richer lives with love in them. But how would we go about showing such a hermit that this is so and that his own life would become richer if he allowed himself to feel connected to other people? Emotional hermits are typically blind to their lack of love. They do not notice their emotional isolation, or if they do, they do not care. So they need something especially effective to convince them that they would have a richer life with love in it.

The strategy most of us would use to try to convince emotional hermits of this is to show them what love is like. We would describe love, both its giving and receiving. We would have them read about love in fiction, nonfiction and poetry. And we would show them actual instances of love, including ones directed their way. What we would want to do is to get them to feel what love is like, so that they can recognize that they also need love.

Using the existential argument for believing in God to try to convince someone to believe in God or to try to induce ourselves to believe in God more deeply is like adopting this strategy to convince the emotional hermit that he needs love. This is because believing in God, like the emotional hermit's recognition, is closely connected to the satisfaction of need. It is not like believing a fact of astrophysics.

BELIEVING IN GOD

Believing in God is not like believing a fact of astrophysics because God is a personal being like us. If God simply served abstract metaphysical functions, then believing in God would not be connected to the satisfaction of needs, or at least not to the satisfaction of very many needs. Deist conceptions of God fall into this category. Aristotle's unmoved mover, for example, on whom the universe eternally depends and who does nothing except think of its own thinking, has little connection to human needs. Aristotle's God does not love humans or suffer when they suffer. It has no knowledge of earthly goings on and has no emotions. It is, indeed, hardly personal, a being that humans could connect to in a personal way. Other deist conceptions of God, though not as impersonal as Aristotle's, also picture God as having little to do with satisfaction of human need. In these other conceptions, God is said to have made the physical universe and then set it on its course, watching it develop but not being involved with it. This kind of God is also too removed from human affairs to be able to connect to many of the needs I described in chapter two.

But a God who is fully personal and who has birthed the universe and continues to be involved with it can connect to human needs. Such a God would have thoughts and emotions, would know the daily affairs of humans, and would care about what they did and what happened to them. Humans could connect to such a God in the same way they connect to each other, namely, through need and emotion.

Believing in such a God would be like the emotional hermit's believing that he would have a richer life with love in it. It would also be like a lover believing in her beloved. A lover's believing in her beloved is both cognitive and noncognitive. The cognitive part of her believing contains beliefs about her beloved, such as that he is gentle and gracious, and the noncognitive part contains feelings and desires, such as being attracted to these qualities and feeling glad when they are exhibited toward her. The emotional hermit who believes that he would have a richer life with love in it is not just believing something cognitive but is also having feelings and desires, among them an attraction to the love. Believing in a personal God, too, is partly cognitive and partly noncognitive. It contains the belief that such a God exists and that this God has certain qualities, along with feelings and desires, and includes an attraction to the qualities and a feeling of gladness because God satisfies certain needs. This is why appealing to satisfaction of need is required to evoke the believing—the believing consists in part of that satisfaction.

This, then, is the response to the objection that the existential argument is irrelevant—believing in God is not like believing in bare facts. An appeal to satisfaction of need is required to produce this different kind of believing. This is the function of the existential argument for believing in God. But there is also a more controversial response to the Irrelevancy Objection and to the Invisible George Objection.

THE OBJECTIVIST THESIS

It is commonly assumed that beliefs, and arguments for them, should not be influenced by what we do or do not want to believe about them. We should not, in other words, let our desires affect what we believe. This common assumption is the reigning scientific and philosophical paradigm. We can call it the objectivist thesis because it says that we must be as objective as we can in matters of belief. We must not let passions, emotions or desires influence us when we are trying to find out whether or not a particular assertion is true, except, of course, for the desire to know what is true. Otherwise, we would not be fair and impartial, and without fairness and impartiality our beliefs are much less likely to be true. This objectivist thesis gives the Irrelevancy Objection and the Invisible George Objection their force.

I want to challenge the objectivist thesis. Sometimes having certain emotions is needed to determine what to believe. The situations in which this is the case are those in which claims are closely connected to human need and emotion in some way. Being an emotional hermit or a lover are instances of such situations, and so is believing in God. Assessing evidence for the legitimacy of believing in God requires having the right emotions. And having these emotions rightly prompts the believing, as the existential argument maintains.

Perhaps the best way to make a case for this claim is through examples. I will start with one involving moral perception, as it is like believing in God in certain respects. I take this case from Lawrence Blum, an American philosopher, in a book on moral perception. Blum writes,

> John and Joan are riding on a subway train, seated. There are no empty seats and some people are standing; yet the subway car is not packed so tightly as to be uncomfortable for everyone. One of the passengers standing is a woman in her thirties holding two relatively full shopping bags. John is not particularly paying attention to the woman, but he is cognizant of her. Joan, by contrast, is distinctly aware that the woman is un-

comfortable. . . . John, let us say, often fails to take in people's discomfort, whereas Joan is characteristically sensitive to such discomfort. It is thus in character for the discomfort to be salient for Joan but not for John. That is to say, a morally significant aspect of situations facing John characteristically fails to be salient for him, and this is a defect of his character. . . . John misses something of the moral reality confronting him. . . . His deficiency is a situational self-absorption or attentional laziness.[5]

Blum uses this case to illustrate two points: (1) John fails to see a feature of the moral reality confronting him, and (2) this failure is due to a deficiency of character. This deficiency is moral, Blum states, for it involves self-absorption and attentional laziness. Attentional laziness is a moral defect in moral contexts, which is what the subway situation is. These two points have positive correlates in Joan: (1) Joan sees a feature of the moral reality confronting her, and (2) this seeing is due to positive moral features of her character—concern for the welfare of others and attentional alertness.

This example makes the point that correct moral perception depends on having the right moral qualities. The objectivist thesis fails to account for the assertion that the passions, emotions and desires involved in having moral qualities are sometimes needed to determine what to believe. The desire to be aware of people's discomfort and pain is needed to observe people being in discomfort or pain. Without this desire, the evidence that is right in front of someone's eyes will not be appreciated, just as the rich man in Jesus' story of the rich man and Lazarus did not appreciate the plight of Lazarus as he passed by him every day (Lk 16:19-31). In the bending light situation, however, the evidence can be seen even though an observer does not have the desire to be aware of other people's discomfort or any other moral desire connected to human need—except, again, for the desire to acquire knowledge fairly and honestly. This is because the bending light situation does not involve human discomfort or human need. Since the subway situation does involve human need, one who is in it must have certain emotions and desires to observe accurately what is going on.

---

[5]Lawrence Blum, *Moral Perception and Particularity* (Cambridge: Cambridge University Press, 1994), pp. 31-33.

The emotional hermit and the lover illustrate the same points. For the emotional hermit to recognize that love would make his life richer, he must appreciate the value of love in his life. And for him to appreciate the value of love in his life, he must actually feel the love. Remember that emotional hermits shut themselves off from love—they do not display affection and feel uncomfortable receiving it. So although they might think that love is valuable for some people, they would not think that they themselves need it. For them to think this, they would have to break through the shell with which they have surrounded themselves to experience what love is like. They would, in other words, have to have certain emotions and desires to know a certain truth about themselves. It is the same for the lover. She values her beloved. She has certain emotions and desires that are directed toward him. As a result, she is more sensitive to his moral qualities. She sees his trustworthiness more readily than does a mere acquaintance. She discerns the subtle ways in which he exercises kindness more quickly than one who cares little about kindness. She notices his compassion, willingness to listen and generosity—all because she cares about compassion, listening and generosity, especially in one she wants to love.

Believing in God is like each of these cases. It is like the moral perception case because believing in God requires moral and spiritual perception akin to Joan's perception of the uncomfortable woman in the subway car. The moral perception required to believe in God is to recognize that the emotional and spiritual needs that are connected to believing in God matter. Without this recognition, one will not be prompted to believe in God because of the needs or be inclined to think of them as evidence for a God who has made humans with such needs.

The way to recognize that the needs matter is simply to feel them. If we feel them, we are going to want them to be satisfied, and if we want them to be satisfied, we are going to regard them as important, especially if they involve cosmic matters, as they do. If John had ever been in distress and needed someone to have compassion on him, he might well have come to recognize the importance of compassion. He might then have begun to notice the distress of others who need compassion. Someone who does not recognize the importance of the needs mentioned in the existential argument for believing in God is not likely to be moved by them to believe in God or to think of the needs as requiring an explanation. But if one does recognize the importance of the needs, one is more likely to be moved by them to believe and to regard them as requiring an explanation. One will be less inclined to accept a naturalistic explanation of them. "They cannot simply be explained away," such a person will say.

The same points hold true in the emotional hermit and lover cases. The emotional hermit needs to feel that love matters to recognize that having it will make his life richer. And the lover needs to value certain qualities in the one she loves to see them in her beloved more readily than other people do. In each of these cases, having certain emotions sharpens one's perception. In sum, the objectivist thesis is false when it comes to cases in which need and emotion are involved. In such cases, possessing certain moral qualities or emotions is necessary for recognizing what one should believe or for recognizing the evidence in favor of a claim. Since believing in God involves satisfying needs, one must have certain moral qualities and emotions to come to believe in God. Having those qualities and emotions prompts the believing.

We can construe the factory girl as exemplifying these points, as she is in a situation like that of the emotional hermit, lover and moral perceiver—what she does or does not believe is closely connected to her emotions and desires. She desperately wants to believe that there is something better than the trouble and distress that she has been experiencing. Let us suppose that she is reflective, and thinks, "Just because I want to believe that there is something better doesn't mean that there actually is something better. Still, it is a curious fact that I have this desire at all, plus other desires involving God and the afterlife." Because she takes her desires seriously, she is led to think of her having the desires as requiring an explanation. Otherwise, it would not have occurred to her that they need an explanation, or if it had, she could well have dismissed the question as being insignificant. So she is led, in this hypothetical reworking of the situation, to supplement her existential reasoning with evidential reasoning because of the emotional force of the existential reasoning.

FAIR AND IMPARTIAL

An advocate of the objectivist thesis will no doubt respond to what I have been saying by asserting that though it may be that people assess evidence differently when they have certain emotions, this does not mean that they should do so. They should be fair and impartial, which means that they need to excise all emotions that influence their assessment of the evidence, as the reigning paradigm in science and philosophy asserts.

One should, indeed, excise all emotions that skew the fair and impartial assessment of evidence. But in the situations I have been describing, the presence of certain emotions is needed to assess evidence fairly and impartially. In the moral perception case, concern for the welfare of others and attentional alertness are needed to perceive that the subway rider is not very comfortable. In the emotional hermit case, the hermit needs to feel love to recognize that his life would be richer with love in it. In the lover case, the lover needs to be attracted to her beloved to observe the subtleties of his positive moral qualities—subtleties that really are in him, not exaggerated or attributed falsely to him just because of the lover's attraction. With respect to believing in God, feeling the needs mentioned in the existential argument for believing in God prompts one to feel their importance and thus that they require an explanation. Having certain emotions in all these cases results in fairness and impartiality instead of undermining them.

EMOTIONS THAT INHIBIT FAIRNESS AND IMPARTIALITY

To reinforce these claims, I shall describe several emotions and moral states that undermine the fair and impartial assessment of evidence, emotions which must be replaced by their positive correlates so that assessment can be fair and impartial. John Henry Newman, the nineteenth century British theologian mentioned above, who concurs with the thesis that believing in God requires having the right moral qualities, mentions two such states: "the allurements of sense and the supremacy of self."[6] These, he says, "enfeeble, obstruct, and pervert" our perception of the

---

[6]John Henry Newman, *An Essay in Aid of a Grammar of Assent*, ed. with introduction and notes by I. T. Ker (Oxford: Oxford University Press, 1985), p. 202.

first principles of truth.[7] One who has these qualities has a different "character of mind" from one who has "aspirations after the supernatural."[8] Both "our moral as well as our intellectual being," Newman states, are part of our character of mind, and thus are involved in knowing the first principles of truth.[9] Newman means to apply this point to believing in God as much as to what he calls the first principles of truth.

How do the allurements of sense obstruct believing in God? Newman does not tell us, but we can imagine how it works. Newman contrasts the allurements of sense with "aspirations after the supernatural." Aspirations after the eternal no doubt include being open to believing in God. So the allurements of sense consist of an attraction to knowledge of the physical world that precludes this openness. One is allured by sense knowledge so much that one is skeptical of anything purporting to show that there is a supernatural realm. This allurement would undermine any attempt to show that God is the source of the existential needs. One would value sense knowledge of the physical world so highly that an inference to a supernatural cause of the existential needs would be automatically suspected, and a natural cause, such as an evolutionary, Freudian or neurological one, would be automatically preferred. What happens, consequently, is that the allurements of sense obstruct the fair and impartial consideration of evidence for believing in God. It needs to be replaced with a willingness to believe in the supernatural should evidence point in that direction.

How does the supremacy of self obstruct believing in God? By the supremacy of self, Newman probably means egotism, selfishness or unwarranted pride, perhaps mixed with a measure of autonomy. This supremacy of self would make one feel that they do not need to depend on God. The existence of God, in fact, would be a threat to the person who possesses supremacy of self. And, clearly, one can hardly be open to believing in God or rightly assessing evidence for believing in God if one finds God a threat. One would be more inclined to think that the needs mentioned in the existential argument for believing in God

---

[7]Ibid.
[8]Ibid.
[9]Ibid.

would be satisfied by natural means instead of supernatural ones. One would be predisposed constantly to look for holes in evidential arguments for believing in God, somewhat like a person who wants to find fault with an acquaintance by constantly looking for errors she makes. Again, this character trait obstructs fairness and impartiality. It must be replaced with a proper humility and a willingness to depend on God should it turn out that there is a God.

Mark Wynn, in his book on emotions and religious understanding, suggests a third moral state that inhibits fair and impartial assessment of evidence for believing in God. He proposes that "theistic experience can be understood (in some cases anyway) as a kind of affectively toned sensitivity to the values that 'make up' God's reality."[10] By "affectively toned sensitivity" he means a sensitivity that is fused with an emotion or attitude, such as Joan's sensitive concern for people in distress. Wynn is suggesting, therefore, that our experience of God depends on having a positive attitude toward the values in God's moral character. Consider a person who does not value forgiveness. She is assertive and aggressive and believes in getting on with life in spite of one's blunders. Forgiveness for her means dwelling too much on guilt, which is entirely too negative for her taste. One should look to future possibilities and not obsess over the past. Such a person will not value the forgiveness God is said to offer and therefore will not be able to experience God as one who forgives. Nor will such a person be inclined to include forgiveness on a list of important emotional and spiritual needs. Consequently, she will not regard the need for forgiveness that some people say they have as rightly prompting faith in God or as evidence for a God who has put that need into humans. Like John on the subway, who does not recognize discomfort because he does not value concern for it, this person will not be in a position to assess fairly and impartially the significance of the need for forgiveness, because she does not value it. Her indifference to it must be replaced with an appreciation of the value of forgiveness if she is to be fair and impartial.

This is not to say that emotion precedes knowledge whenever the

---

[10]Mark R. Wynn, *Emotional Experience and Religious Understanding: Integrating Perception, Conception and Feeling* (Cambridge: Cambridge University Press, 2005), p. 5.

two interact, that is, that one always has a certain emotion before coming to know something. In some cases the reverse might be true, namely, that knowledge produces emotion. In the subway case, for example, it might be that John acquires an emotional disposition toward the discomfort of other subway riders through an acknowledgement of a version of the Golden Rule: If we want people to notice our discomfort, we should notice their discomfort. In general, we can say that sometimes emotion comes first and sometimes knowledge comes first. And sometimes the two are so intertwined that it is impossible to say which comes first.[11] As things stood with John, however, he needed to have an emotion before coming to appreciate someone's distress. And people need to possess the right emotions to believe in God.

This, then, is another response to the Irrelevancy Objection and the Invisible George Objection: people need the proper emotions to recognize certain truths. In particular, acquiring the beliefs that God exists and cares for humans requires certain emotions. The objectivist thesis embodied in the Irrelevancy Objection and the Invisible George Objection is mistaken. So the existential argument for believing in God does not, in the end, succumb to them.

CONCLUSION

Although the Invisible George Objection to the existential argument for believing in God is right, the argument still has a role to play in acquiring faith—first, when it is supplemented with the belief that God exists; second, when it is combined with the evidential use of need to ground faith; third, when it is realized that believing in God is connected to the satisfaction of need; and fourth, when it is understood that having certain emotions is needed to assess rightly evidence for believing in God.

---

[11]For a discussion of which comes first in a slightly different context, see Alvin Plantinga, *Warranted Christian Belief* (New York: Oxford University Press, 2000), pp. 295-304. Plantinga's conclusion is that the two are often so intertwined that it is impossible to say which comes first: "The structure of will and intellect here is perhaps a spiral, dialectical process. . . . There are certain things you won't know unless you love, have the right affections; there are certain affections you won't have without perceiving some of God's moral qualities; neither perceiving nor affection can be said to be prior to the other" (pp. 303-4).

These four possibilities support my thesis that both need and reason are required to support faith. Using reason ensures that need will not blindly attach itself to questionable objects; feeling need ensures that reason will not be sterile. Need draws us to faith in God because faith in God includes satisfaction of need. Need also provokes emotions that reason must have to operate rightly. The bottom line is that we are creatures with both reason and need, and faith in God is connected to both. This means that neither logical rationality nor need rationality alone is sufficient for faith in God. The two must coalesce.

The following account involves both need and reason. Susan was in her early twenties when I recorded these words.

SUSAN: BECOMING REAL

I grew up in a Christian family, and somehow I have the ability to figure out what people want me to be and then become that. My theory is that I was being spiritual because that was in my environment.

For example, I led a prayer ministry because I thought that the way I could be accepted in my social environment was to be strongly spiritual. I felt I was always striving to feel something that I saw other people experiencing. I saw the things they did. They prayed, they read their Bibles, they felt things during worship, and I decided I should do those things too. So I did. The deeper I got, the more it looked as if I was doing okay spiritually.

I wasn't deliberately trying to deceive people. I think mostly I was trying to convince myself that I was a Christian. I wanted so much to believe Christianity and become a Christian. I wanted to become someone who is deeply affected by God, by Christ, by whatever it is in Christianity that changes people, because I saw that it made people happy.

Six months ago I was having a conversation with a friend, and she asked me the old classic, "If you died tonight, would you go to heaven? If someone held a gun to your head and said, 'Do you believe that Jesus is the Son of God?' what would you say?" I don't know why, but it was a really honest moment. I hesitated for so long. I didn't know. So I realized, "I have enough courage now, it's time for me to face my doubts."

That moment of honesty came from something that had happened in a Thursday evening prayer service. I remembered a time when my family told me we were moving, and I remembered sitting in my room and crying. I was hurt and I didn't want to leave people I knew. I knew my mom was outside my room, but I felt that she didn't care. My dad was nowhere to be found. I felt abandoned. When I remembered these things at the prayer service, I fell to my knees—I literally couldn't stand anymore. It brought up so much pain and so many other memories that I got freaked out. Then I got angry at God and felt abandoned by God. Somehow it all spiraled back to the core of Christianity and what I believed about it. I didn't know.

In a short series of weeks, I stopped being in the prayer ministry, I stopped giving people the impression that I could lead them spiritually, I stopped acting the same way during worship. I stopped engaging. I sat back and listened and watched and thought, "Okay, what's going on, and do I really buy into this?"

For the first couple of weeks, maybe even for the first couple of months, the entire foundation of my world was ripped apart, because so much of who I was had been based on the Christian subculture. You pray, you read your Bible, you're a Christian, and that's how things are. If my beliefs were ripped away, I couldn't act on them any more with integrity. Integrity is really important to me. So I stopped engaging in all those things and went through upheaval in my life.

I cried every day for three or four months. I stopped praying. I was still reading my Bible, but skeptically. "What is this? God made Adam and Eve leave the Garden of Eden, but he put them there in the first place?" All the questions I had repressed for my whole life were now high in the forefront of my brain. Did the resurrection happen? Did Jesus live? How do I know? I went back to questioning the very nature of reality. What's real? How do I know? Do I feel loved? Questions like that.

The upheaval climaxed right after the incident six months ago. I couldn't sleep. I couldn't eat. I stopped working out. I still went to church, but it was more so I could have a setting where I could ask people questions. I was in pain, but I had no idea why. There was a point when I was hanging out with a friend and I cried for two and half hours, because my pain was so deep that I couldn't identify where it was coming from. I stayed awake at night scared that I was going to go to hell. I condemned myself because I felt as if I was going to walk away from my faith. My entire life would be different; I would do drugs, I would rebel, I would go off the deep end.

There were times when I was low enough to commit suicide. It wasn't a plan—if I hit this point, I will do this. It was more that when I'd be in the kitchen and there'd be a knife, I would think, "I could cut my wrist." I was a big mess on the inside—a big ball of pain and emotions, wanting to express myself.

I don't know how I got past this stage. I just plowed through it. I kept going. People asked about me and expressed that they cared, and I had the hope that I'd solve it somehow, that eventually there'd be enough of a foundation for me to live.

I've found parts of the foundation. I've found enough that I'm not in extremely poignant emotional pain in every part of my life or incapacitated. I've found that I believe that the reality that we see and touch and feel is real. I've found that there is a God, and he communicates with people, some people, and he created the world. Going out into nature is a huge part of my foundation. I can't look at a tree or a plant, especially mountains, and think that they just happened.

I wouldn't call myself a Christian, but I still go to church, because people there let me ask questions. When my faith, my pseudo faith, whatever I had until six months ago, collapsed, I still wanted to be a Christian. I feel as if I'm working my way back to that. But for it to be an honest journey, it has to be very real for me not to be a Christian. I can't take communion, because I can't in good conscience take a piece of bread and drink wine that represents Jesus' blood and body and mean something significant that changed my life, because I haven't experienced that. I don't pray very often. I've pretty much stopped reading my Bible.

I wouldn't say it's just intellectual questions, although that's a big part of it. It's mostly emotional pain, I think. I've been very wounded. This is hard for me to admit, but I need to. It has affected my spiritual life and my view of God.

I feel very emotionally abandoned by my family, particularly by my dad. He's such a hard person on the outside. On the inside he loves people, but he never lets it out. So he can't—or won't—reach me on that. Because of that, when I'm honest about why I'm hurt, when I'm praying especially, I'll sense God and be angry. "You have abandoned me. You brought so much pain into my life. You bring pain into people's lives all the time. I hate that, and I hate you for that."

The image of God and the image of my dad are melded together in my head, and I can't separate them. I expect God to act with me and feel toward me as my dad acts and feels toward me. I react to God on that basis most of the time. I think that's the core of this whole thing. The reason I'm not able to have faith is because of the intellectual questions and this emotional pain.

Since that time six months ago, I've had a fairly joyless existence. But I have hope, even faith, that this stage of my life is temporary and that there might be a God out there who loves me, who even loves me unconditionally. I have hope that this God might be the same God of a Palestinian man named Jesus who lived under the rule of the Roman Empire in AD 30. Who was this man and what is all the hoopla about him? That is a fun question.

Both intellectual and emotional elements are prominent in Susan's re-evaluation of the faith in which she grew up. She wants to know whether important elements of that faith are true. Was there really a Jesus, and why do people make so much of him? Is there a God who made everything? If so, why did this God put people into a perfect environment only to kick them out later? At the same time, she is very much disturbed about something but doesn't know exactly what it is at first. She tumbles to her knees, she cries endlessly, she stops eating, she thinks about killing herself. Upon reflection, she realizes that she has been emotionally starved. She feels abandoned by her parents, especially her father, who has not been as warm and connected as she has needed him to be. She also feels abandoned by God and is angry at God. Yet she hopes that somehow she can acquire a real faith to replace the pretense in which she had been living.

The kind of faith Susan is looking for would have to be true, and it would have to satisfy her desperate need to be loved. Her story shows that sometimes reason and satisfaction of need are clearly distinguished.

5

OBJECTION TWO

THE EXISTENTIAL ARGUMENT
JUSTIFIES BELIEF IN ANY KIND OF GOD

IF THE EXISTENTIAL ARGUMENT FOR BELIEVING in God is sound, would it not also justify believing in an invisible cosmic tyrant who likes to torture humans with murder, starvation, political oppression and the like? This is the question behind the second objection to the existential argument. It says that basing belief in God solely on the satisfaction of need is illegitimate because it would also justify believing in any kind of God. If someone felt a need to believe in a God that had the personality of one of the Greek gods, such as Aphrodite, Dionysus or Zeus, then the reasoning in the existential argument would justify them in doing so. And if someone felt a need to believe in a God who tortured humans gratuitously, then they would be justified in believing in a cosmic tyrant. The reasoning would be analogous to that in the existential argument for believing in God:

1. I have a need for there to be gratuitous torture of humans.

2. Believing in a cosmic being, Tyrant George, who tortures humans gratuitously, satisfies this need.

3. Therefore, I am justified in believing in Tyrant George.

The heart of this objection is the same as that of the Invisible George Objection: we cannot rely solely on satisfaction of need to support faith in God. If we do, our believing will be faulty, for we can just as well believe in something that does not exist, such as Invisible George, or in something that is perverse, such as Tyrant George.

The correct response to this objection is the same as to the Invisible George Objection—it is right. The existential argument cannot be trusted as it stands. However, as with the Invisible George Objection, this is not all that can be said. Although satisfaction of need by itself does not warrant believing in God, reason and need together do.

WHAT NEEDS?

As it stands, the existential argument for believing in God does not contain criteria for excluding the need to torture. The most obvious criterion to add and thereby rule out this "need" is simply to require that good, not evil, needs be used to justify believing in God. They cannot be morally suspect, corrupt or immoral. This is so because a God who is evil would not really be God and would not be worthy of being believed in. Adopting this added criterion is like saying that we would not believe that a message is from God if it violated our deepest moral convictions. Terrorists, for example, who claimed that God commands them on a suicide mission would be mistaken because God would not command anyone to kill like that. Similarly, we would be disinclined to believe an argument purporting to show that God is perverse based on the supposed need for torture.

This response will seem intuitively obvious to most people. To objectors, however, it will not. They will say that the advocates of the existential argument have begged the question. They have simply assumed the falsity of the conclusion that the Tyrant George Argument purports to establish.

I do not think that the objectors' reply is adequate, for our intuitive conviction about the goodness of needs seems to me to be objectively right. Nevertheless, I shall give another response to the Tyrant George Objection that does not rely on that conviction. I will propose five criteria that needs must meet for them to be included in the existential argument. These criteria are independently acceptable, that is, acceptable on grounds other than that they rule out the need for torture. But they do in fact rule it out. I shall call them the need criteria.

The need criteria

1. Needs must be felt by many others; in fact, they must be felt by most people, if not all. They cannot just be my needs or even the needs of a particular group of people.

2. Needs must endure. They cannot be fleeting, but must return again and again. (Otherwise, we would call them whims.)

3. Needs must be significant. They cannot be trivial or superficial.

4. Needs must be part of a constellation of connected needs, each of which meets the other criteria. They cannot be isolated, that is, unconnected to any of our other needs or other parts of our character.

5. Needs must be felt strongly. They cannot be ones that we can take or leave indifferently.

These five criteria rule out the "need" for torture, because it is not felt by many people, does not endure, and is not part of a constellation of connected needs. We can, of course, imagine a hypothetical world in which the need for torture met all five conditions. In such a world, all or nearly all of the human race would feel the need strongly and often. And the humans in this hypothetical world would have other needs that Tyrant George, or only Tyrant George, would satisfy. If there were such a race of humans, then the existential argument, with these five criteria, would justify having faith in a perverse God. The point, however, is to explain actually existing needs. As things stand in the current reality, the need for torture does not meet all of the five criteria. There are, to be sure, people who feel a strong desire for torture, but not enough, not their entire lives, and not part of an integrated character, for this to be a basis for faith in a perverse God.

The thirteen needs I described in chapter two do meet the five criteria. Many people have had them in a variety of cultures. They are not afternoon whims, but return from time to time to energize or to haunt. Nor are they trivial and superficial, but are felt at the deepest levels of our character. Each need is connected to some of the others, and together they form an integrated group. In addition, they are felt strongly, at least some of the time by some people.

A DEFENSE OF THE CRITERIA

Can we go one step further and explain why these criteria are independently acceptable? I think we can. They are, first of all, the criteria that are used in assessing reports of unusual phenomena. If someone claims to have seen a new species of lion in an African desert, hitherto unreported in the literature on lions, we require corroborating sightings by others before giving full assent to the claim. We also want the sightings to be made in optimal conditions so that we can be sure no mistake had been made. These requirements involve the first two criteria and the last one. In addition, we would want to know how the new species differs from other species and what its habitat is, plus other information that connects it to what we know about lions. This involves the fourth criterion—information is more reliable if it is connected to other information.

Second, the criteria are used in examining circumstantial evidence presented in courtrooms. One bit of circumstantial evidence does not have as much strength as a number of such bits that are connected to each other. If several people report similar information about a defendant's whereabouts at the time of the crime, the plausible explanation has more weight than if just one person gives such information. Information that is more centrally connected to important features of the crime also has more weight. These involve the first, third and fourth criteria—evidence is stronger if it is given by more than one person, is significant, and is connected to other evidence.

Third, psychologists who construct theories of personality have tried to take into account needs and desires that fit all of the five criteria. Their aim has been to find a central organizing idea that explains these needs and desires. For Alfred Adler this idea was the drive for power; for Ernest Becker it was the drive for immortality projects; for existential psychiatry it is the drive for meaning. The needs and desires they try to explain by these central ideas are ones they believe everyone has, ones that endure throughout one's life, are deeply significant, are connected to other needs and desires, and are strongly felt. A personality theory not based on such needs and desires, these theorists believe, would not accurately represent who we really are.

So the five criteria are commonly used in various domains as tests of what is acceptable and what is not. They are not, to be sure, precise and exact. But the domains in which they operate are rarely precise and exact either. Sometimes, in fact, the application of the criteria is rather imprecise, calling us to weigh alternatives and judge which criteria should be given more weight. This imprecision is a common condition in courtrooms, the advance of science, and constructing theories of the universe. Still, in spite of the imprecision in the criteria, we rely on them in a wide variety of situations to distinguish between what is worthy of belief and what is not. With respect to belief in God, we use the criteria to demarcate "needs" that we decidedly would never think of using to justify faith in a God from needs that we do think justify faith in God.

TRUSTING NEEDS

Imagine again the scenario in which a fully formed, adult human is created and placed in a sea of wildflowers. Let us suppose that she is sinless. All of her desires are good—to explore the wildflowers, gaze at the deep blue expanse of the sky, love God and experience awe of God. Perhaps it would be more accurate to call the desires that are connected to God impulses, for "desire" (and "need") presuppose that one feels a lack, and the sinless state I am imagining is "full" as well as without sin. Eve's impulse to experience awe of God is fully satisfied by her actually having awe of God. Her impulse is not like the desire or longing for awe that we currently experience, which is unmistakably accompanied by an awareness of our lack of awe.

Can Eve trust her impulses to justify having faith in God? I believe she can. She would not have to appeal to the five criteria to see which of her impulses she could trust. She would instinctively trust them. It would be a matter of course with her and not one of examination and reflection, as it would be if she were to employ the criteria and go through the steps in the existential argument for believing in God. She would not first say to herself, "I have an impulse to experience awe of God," then "Faith in God satisfies this impulse," and conclude with "I am justified in having faith in God." Rather, she would intuitively and naturally move from impulse to faith.

We, however, not being in a sinless state, must examine and reflect. We cannot trust our impulses, desires and needs in the way Eve does. We must employ reason to weed out the perverse ones. But just because we cannot trust our needs as Eve does, it does not follow that we cannot trust them at all. We trust them when they are conjoined with reason— the reasonableness that is exemplified in the five need criteria along with the uses of reason described in the last chapter.

THE EVIDENTIAL ARGUMENT AGAIN

The five criteria also play a role in the evidential argument for believing in God based on need. Consider circumstantial evidence. The five criteria rule out weak circumstantial evidence, and they also tell us when we have strong evidence. If evidence satisfies four or five of the criteria to a high degree, we give it credence—a defendant is convicted, the cat down the street got the baby birds, Mr. Konrad was the one who left the anonymous message. It is the same with the thirteen existential needs. They cannot be dismissed on the grounds that only a few isolated people experience them or that they are afternoon whims. Nor can they be written off with the charge that they are insignificant, unconnected to any other need or barely felt. Many people experience them throughout their lives. They are significant, form a connected group and are felt strongly. So they require an explanation. The explanation that first comes to mind is that God puts them into us, as God is the central focus of the needs. If there is no better explanation, such as might be given by evolutionary psychology or the Freudian unconscious, then we should accept this first one.

THE TEST OF PRACTICAL RATIONALITY

The existential argument for believing in God passes what William James calls the test of "practical rationality." James asks, "Can we define the tests of rationality which those parts of our nature would use?"[1] The parts of our nature he has in mind are the practical parts. He does

---

[1]William James, "The Sentiment of Rationality," in *The Writings of William James*, ed. John J. McDermott (New York: Modern Library, 1968), p. 325.

not tell us what counts as a practical part of our nature, but clearly indicates that it contains desires, impulses and emotions rather than logical reasoning. The claim James makes with respect to the practical part of our nature is that a philosophy must not disappoint the desires, impulses and emotions in it: the "ultimate principle [of a philosophy] must not be one that essentially baffles and disappoints our dearest desires and most cherished powers."[2] An example of a philosophy that does baffle and disappoint our dearest desires, according to James, is materialism, the view that everything is made up only of matter and is ruled entirely by natural laws. Materialism, James says, "denies reality to the objects of almost all the impulses which we cherish." The impulses and emotions he has in mind are "fortitude, hope, rapture, admiration, earnestness, and the like." We enjoy reacting with these emotions, but "very unwillingly react with fear, disgust, despair, or doubt." So "a philosophy which should only legitimate emotions of the latter sort would be sure to leave the mind a prey to discontent and craving."[3] And this, James believes, would justify rejecting that philosophy.

James's reasoning goes something like this:

> A philosophy must not baffle and disappoint our dearest desires and most cherished powers. But materialism does this, because it does not allow us to exercise the virtues of fortitude, hope, rapture, admiration and earnestness, and we dearly want to exercise these virtues. So materialism should be rejected.

This reasoning is like the existential argument for believing in God, as it argues that materialism should be rejected because it is unsatisfying to us. The test of practical rationality that the argument employs is the first statement: A philosophy must not thwart the satisfaction of our dearest desires or frustrate the employment of our most cherished powers.

James's test of practical rationality is somewhat like my five need criteria, for its aim is to give us a way of determining what desires should be satisfied when believing a particular philosophy. It rules out satisfy-

---

[2]Ibid., p. 328.
[3]Ibid., pp. 329-30.

ing only negative desires and says that positive ones should be satisfied. As such, it says something like my fourth criterion for acceptable needs, namely, that needs must be part of a constellation of connected needs, not isolated and disconnected. The negative emotions James mentions—fear, disgust, despair and doubt—are not well integrated into one's personality. In addition, James's test of practical rationality, like my five criteria, is commonly used in a variety of conditions. We accept it as a principle that rules out certain desires as unworthy of affecting what we believe and as allowing other desires to affect what we believe. Using it, along with my five criteria, answers the Tyrant George Objection to the existential argument for believing in God.

WISHFUL THINKING?

One might dismiss James's test of practical rationality as a simple appeal to wishful thinking, as he favors positive emotions such as hope, rapture and admiration rather than negative ones such as fear and disgust. Why should one not favor negative emotions and infer that a tyrant who likes to make us fear and experience disgust rules the world? James's rejection of materialism on the grounds that it makes us "discontent and craving" is an obvious appeal to desire, an objector might say. But desire is notoriously unreliable in determining what to believe.

A COMPLEX APPEAL TO DESIRE

James's argument certainly looks as if it is a simple appeal to desire. However, interpreting it as a complex appeal to desire fits what James says better.

First, the virtues James appeals to—fortitude, hope, rapture, admiration, earnestness and the like—do not fit neatly into an "I like this" mode, that is, they are not for something that benefits us. Most of them are more like the other-directed needs I described in chapter two—the need to experience awe, to delight in goodness and to love. Admiration of other people is like these other-directed desires, and so is earnestness. We need admiration and earnestness, but not for the same reason we need to satisfy our self-directed needs, such as for cosmic security and forgiveness. With unsatisfied self-directed needs, we would not possess something we want to possess, but with unsatisfied other-directed needs we would not be the kind of person we want to be. So James's argument is not a simple appeal to wish fulfillment, as Freud supposed all belief in God resulted from, but is more like an appeal to self-realization. The satisfaction involved is not a simple, "It benefits me," but is something like, "This encourages me to be my truest self," or "This encourages me to live up to my highest ideals." Believing in Tyrant George does not do this sort of encouraging.

Second, James's argument asserts that some philosophies are intimately connected to human desires; if the philosophies do not allow for the satisfaction of those desires, they should be rejected. The wishful thinking objector denies this assertion by stating that no philosophies are connected to human desires. That is, no philosophies should be decided on the basis of whether they allow desires to be satisfied. Reality, they say, is what it is independently of human desires. This last assertion seems so obviously true that one wonders how James can support his contention that there is a connection between some philosophies and human desires. Here is how he might do it.

The crucial idea is that some philosophies contain the claim that believing in them satisfies certain desires. Other philosophies do not contain such assertions, and they are the ones for which the wishful thinking objector is right—believing them is not designed to satisfy any desires. But some philosophies are designed to satisfy desires. The "religious hypothesis" is such a philosophy, according to James. The religious hypothesis is, first, that "the best things are the more eternal things," and, second, that "we are better off even now if we believe her first affirmation to be true."[4] So, James would say, believing the religious hypothesis is closely connected to desires, in particular, desires for the best things. This means that the test of practical rationality is applicable to it.

Theism, which is more robust than James's religious hypothesis, is

---

[4] William James, "The Will to Believe," in *The Writings of William James*, ed. John J. McDermott (New York: Modern Library, 1968), pp. 731-32. It is not clear that James believed in traditional theism, but he does seem to believe in "the religious hypothesis" or something like it, for he applies his formula for believing in "The Will to Believe" to the religious hypothesis and finds that it is acceptable (pp. 732-33).

also connected to desires. Not only does it tell us that God exists (which is, indeed, the case independently of human desires), but it tells us that believing in God satisfies our need for cosmic security: God will take care of us, come what may. Theism contains further desire claims as well, such as that believing in God satisfies our desire to know something that is perfectly good, that believing in God satisfies our desire for meaning, and more. These connections of theism with desires mean that the test of practical rationality is also applicable to it.

Theism and the religious hypothesis have an advantage over believing in Tyrant George, for believing in Tyrant George does not satisfy the full range of human desires and emotions. The cosmic tyrant philosophy—that there is a cosmic tyrant who takes glee in inflicting gratuitous pain on innocent and defenseless humans—does, indeed, contain a desire claim. Believe in the cosmic tyrant, it says, and you will have your desire for seeing people suffer gratuitously satisfied. Some people may have this desire. In fact, many people may have temporarily harbored the desire (which they probably would not want to admit). So believing in a cosmic tyrant fulfills the test of practical rationality for at least some people—but only to a degree even for them. For the desire to see people suffer gratuitously is not one of our "dearest" desires, as James put it: the "ultimate principle [of a philosophy] must not be one that essentially baffles and disappoints our dearest desires." We have other desires which conflict with the gratuitous harm desire and which we regard as dearer to us. They are dearer because they satisfy the second, third, fourth and fifth criteria of the five need criteria I set out earlier. They endure, are significant, are part of a constellation of interconnected needs and are felt more strongly. They are, in short, a more central part of our character. Accordingly, theism and James's religious hypothesis pass the test of practical rationality better than the cosmic tyrant philosophy does. And, I might add, theism passes it better than James's religious hypothesis, as there are more ways in which it is satisfactorily connected to desires.

Third, James does not say that the test of practical rationality is the only test a philosophy must pass to be believed. He does not say that we can believe a philosophy that passes the test of practical rationality even though there is good evidence that the philosophy is false, that is, that desire wins when reason is pitted against it. Nor does he say that we can believe a philosophy for which there is no evidence either way just because it passes the test of practical rationality (that is, that desire is sufficient when there is no reason to believe). James's quotations above from "The Sentiment of Rationality" say only that a philosophy intimately connected to human desire must past the test of practical rationality. This means merely that the test is a necessary condition for believing. It does not mean that the test is the only necessary condition or that it is a sufficient condition for believing. It may be that possessing some evidence is also a necessary condition for believing. If so, one should not believe simply because doing so satisfies one's desires, which means that one should not believe in Tyrant George or God simply because of desire. But believing in God both because it satisfies desires and because there is good reason to do so is legitimate.

In sum, the existential argument for believing in God is not a simple need or desire argument. Because of this, it is stronger than either the Invisible George or the Tyrant George objection make it out to be.

FREUD AND WISH-FULFILLMENT

This conclusion differs from Sigmund Freud's dismissal of religious belief, but it also agrees with Freud's views in one respect. Freud asserted that belief in God came from the desire to have a cosmic protector: "religious ideas have arisen from the same need as have all the other achievements of civilization: from the necessity of defending oneself against the crushingly superior force of nature."[5] Because of their origin, religious ideas, Freud says, are illusions: "religious ideas . . . are not precipitates of experience or end-results of thinking: they are illusions, fulfillments of the oldest, strongest and most urgent wishes of mankind."[6] "An illusion," he continues, "is not the same thing as an error. . . . We call a belief an illusion when a wish-fulfillment is a prominent factor in its motivation, and in doing so we disregard its relations

---

[5]Sigmund Freud, *The Future of an Illusion* in *The Freud Reader,* ed. Peter Gay (New York: W. W. Norton, 1989), p. 697.
[6]Ibid., p. 703.

to reality."[7] This means that we cannot say that religious beliefs are true: "No one can be compelled to think them true, to believe in them."[8] But neither can we say they are false just because they have their origin in wishes. We set aside their relation to reality, that is, make no judgment about their truth or falsity.

The first point to notice about Freud's account of religious ideas is that he says they all spring from just one desire—for protection from cosmic harm. This is what I have called "cosmic security" in chapter two. Here I think that Freud has failed to notice that there are other desires that contribute to faith in God, as the accounts in this book show, and as the accounts in such books as William James's *The Varieties of Religious Experience* and classic spiritual autobiographies show. It is almost as if he did not actually look at such accounts or ask people about their religious desires. One gets the impression that Freud is trying to fit an account of faith into his psychological theory. His theory is that every child has Oedipal desires, which include a desire for a strong father. The Oedipus complex, Freud says, is a "universal obsessional neurosis."[9] And the desire for a cosmic protector comes from it: "like the obsessional neurosis of children, it [religion] arose out of the Oedipus complex, out of the relation to the father."[10] It is hard to imagine, however, how a desire for awe or heaven or goodness or most of the other desires described in chapter two can come from Oedipal desires. The correct procedure is to look at the desires from which faith in God actually arises and to construct a theory based on those ways, rather than to try to force those ways into one's already adopted theory, as Freud seems to have done.

The second point to notice is that Freud states that all religious ideas derive just from desire. On this he is on better ground, for many accounts of acquiring faith in God mention desire or need as a motivation for faith, as the ones in this book do. But there are also a good many instances of people acquiring faith without apparently having had a

[7] Ibid., p. 704.
[8] Ibid., p. 705.
[9] Ibid., p. 713.
[10] Ibid.

previous desire for faith, conscious or unconscious.[11] The people to whom this happens often find themselves having a religious experience that simply comes to them, without their trying to induce it or without their having a predisposition toward it. And there are a good many instances of people acquiring faith at least partly as a result of thinking, sometimes just of thinking. So, again, Freud has failed to look at actual instances of people acquiring faith.

The third point to notice is that Freud is careful not to draw the conclusion that religious ideas are false just because they are a product of desire. He has sometimes been misinterpreted as saying this, and has been both commended and criticized for doing so. Unfortunately, Freud's use of "illusion," which has the connotation of being an error, has contributed to this misinterpretation, and Freud sometimes seems to talk in this way. But a careful reading shows that he did not make this elementary mistake, often called the genetic fallacy—the fallacy of inferring that a claim is false because of the fallacious way in which it is derived. He admits that a belief in God could be correct even if it were a product solely of a generally faulty way of supporting beliefs. He is right to say this. But he adds, also rightly, that we would not be justified in adopting such a belief.

This conclusion, however, is not the end of the matter. For there are a number of ways in which faith in God can be supported by reason and thinking. Freud considers a few of these ways, but his considerations are short and inadequate from the perspective of believer and unbeliever alike.[12] They lack a more thorough treatment of reasons believers have given for faith—the best reasons by the best thinkers. They fail to consider the tests of practical rationality above, and they do not deal with the claim that a need for a cosmic protector can serve as an evidential foundation for belief in God (in one of the ways I described in chapter three).

There is a further point to notice. Freud's claim that belief in God is

---

[11]See the numerous accounts in George Wall, *Religious Experience and Religious Belief* (Lanham, Md.: University Press of America, 1995), esp. "The Explanation from Desire and from Unconscious Motivation," pp. 89-141.

[12]Freud, *Future of an Illusion* in *Freud Reader*, pp. 701-3.

derived from Oedipal desires means that it is unhealthy, one that is not good for psychological and emotional well-being. It is, he says, an "obsessional neurosis." This means that we should want to be rid of the belief. But if I am right in saying that faith in God is derived, at least sometimes, from the existential needs described in chapter two, then it is not unhealthy. For satisfying those needs promotes emotional well-being rather than undermines it. This, at any rate, needs to be looked into more empirically than Freud seems to have done. I shall not spend time doing that, but simply look briefly at one prominent psychologist who differs from Freud on the issue.

CARL JUNG AND HEALING EXPERIENCE

Carl Jung became a friend and disciple of Freud but later broke with Freud over key points in Freud's psychology. One of the assertions Jung made that Freud disliked was that religious experience could contribute to emotional well-being. Jung wrote, "No matter what the world thinks about religious experience, the one who has it possesses the great treasure of a thing that has provided him with a source of life, meaning and beauty that has given a new splendor to the world and to mankind."[13] If, he continues, "a healing religious experience . . . helps to make your life healthier, more beautiful, more complete and more satisfactory to yourself and to those you love, you may safely say: 'This was the grace of God.'"[14] Jung is saying three things in these statements. First, religious experience can contribute to emotional health. Second, it does so by bringing meaning to a person, along with beauty and splendor, completeness and satisfaction. Third, the person to whom religious experience brings these features is justified in believing that the way in which the features were acquired is legitimate. It is legitimate because the features are desirable. Having religious experience, then, is good because it produces a good result.

Freud would say that we are not justified in believing in God just because doing so contributes to our happiness, for truth is not discovered by what contributes to our happiness or fulfills our wishes. Jung,

---

[13]Carl Jung, *Psychology and Religion* (New Haven, Conn.: Yale University Press, 1938), p. 113.
[14]Ibid., p. 114.

however, states that Freud has committed the error of "psychologism," which is the error of saying that "if God is anything, he must be an illusion derived from certain motives, from fear, for instance, from will to power, or from repressed sexuality."[15] But, Jung counters, those who derive their belief in God from religious experience are justified in the belief if the experience and the belief help them to live well. The experience, Jung says, produces faith, plus the meaning, beauty, satisfaction and splendor that contribute to emotional health. And, Jung asks, "Where is the *criterium* [criterion] by which you could say that such a life is not legitimate, that such experience is not valid and that such *pistis* [faith] is mere illusion? Is there, as a matter of fact, any better truth about ultimate things than the one that helps you to live?"[16]

In these quotes from Jung, we find something like the existential argument for believing in God. He is saying that because we need meaning, beauty, satisfaction and splendor, and because belief in God helps us to acquire these, we are justified in having that belief. Jung also put this argument in terms of healing neuroses, which after all, is his concern as a working psychologist. When put in these terms, the argument becomes,

1. We want to be healed of our neuroses.

2. Believing in God helps heal our neuroses.

3. Therefore, we are justified in believing in God.

Believing in God helps heal our neuroses because it gives us meaning, beauty, completeness, satisfaction and splendor.

Introducing the concept of healing into the question of whether religious belief is justified gives a deeper dimension to the issue. It is deeper because our neuroses are connected to our basic desires and emotions, such as desires for meaning and love and our fears of rejection and death. The argument says that we are justified in having a belief that heals us of our distress concerning these basic desires and emotions. It is not the simple wish-fulfillment argument Freud criti-

---

[15]Ibid., p. 103. Jung seems to use "illusion" in this quote as "error." This misinterpretation will not affect what I say.
[16]Ibid., pp. 113-14.

cized, but is more like the complex desire argument that William James espoused. It satisfies the five aforementioned criteria for testing whether needs are legitimate. The neuroses Jung says belief in God heals involve desires and emotions that endure, are significant, are connected to one another and are felt strongly. On these grounds, then, the Jungian argument gains force, because it involves an appeal to both need and reason.

Now let us do a thought-experiment. Let us imagine that Freud concedes to Jung that believing in God heals us of our neuroses. (We will need to stretch our imagination a good deal to do this thought-experiment!) It does so in the way Jung suggests, by giving us meaning, beauty, completeness, satisfaction and splendor. Believing in God is not a result simply of a desire for cosmic security or of an obsessional neurosis, as Freud originally thought. The question is this: Will Freud now admit that believing in God is legitimate because it heals us of our neuroses? This will be a troublesome question for Freud. On the one hand, he has declared that we cannot believe something just because it satisfies us. On the other hand, believing in God because it heals us of our neuroses is much more complex and involves deeper parts of our personality than simply wanting to believe. Such complex believing seems more justified than believing because of simple wanting or because of an Oedipus desire. So it should appeal to Freud, as it does to Jung, because he wants patients to be healed, and whatever works to do this presumably is worthy of being believed.

This dilemma is the dilemma of this book: satisfaction of need by itself does not warrant belief in God, yet somehow satisfaction of need seems legitimately to draw us to belief in God. How, then, can we use satisfaction of need to believe in God if satisfaction of need is not in general an acceptable foundation of true beliefs? The answer, I believe, is to accept both the drawing power of need (when it is certified by the need criteria) and its evidential force. In Jung's terms, we acknowledge that belief in God can heal our neuroses and accept this as both existential and evidential justification for the belief. Evidential justification is involved because the ability to be healed by believing in God needs to be explained, and the best explanation is that there is a God who does the healing. It is possible that Jung had in mind both the existential and evidential force of the ability to be healed by believing in God when he asked rhetorically whether there is "any better truth about ultimate things than the one that helps you to live." The real Freud did not accord either existential or evidential force to this ability (which he also did not admit), but perhaps my hypothetical Freud would. In any case, I do, and because of this I believe that we can trust our needs to lead us to faith, or as Jung might put it, that we can trust the religious experiences that heal us to lead us to faith.

Here is another account of acquiring faith. It shows again that need and reason intertwine.

KATHLEEN: TWISTS AND TURNS

I wasn't raised in church. My parents aren't religious. They believe that if people believe in God, that's fine—just have your own beliefs and don't allow them to affect anybody else.

My mom was an alcoholic. When I was five years old, we were coming home from a family party where she had a lot to drink. We were driving on the expressway, my dad was driving, and my mom was in the passenger seat. My mom opened up the door and was about to jump out, but my dad grabbed her by the hair. That made me feel like she didn't love me enough to want to live. From that time on, I didn't trust her, didn't need her as much, and I distanced myself from her.

When I was in fourth grade, my friend Allison invited me to go on a religious retreat with her. My mom said, "Okay, you can go, as long as you don't join a cult." So I went and had a good time. But in my mind I had the same mentality as my mom. "I'm going to go and have fun, and their religious beliefs aren't going to affect me." I went to the retreats once or twice a year for the next three years.

When I was in fourth grade, I began to have certain thoughts that were seemingly not of myself. A word started occurring in my head. It was "rape." It wasn't anything I desired to do, but it felt evil that the word was within me. I knew what the word meant, but I didn't understand it fully. I had never been molested or anything. But just having it exist within my mind made me feel guilty. I thought, "Why would I ever think of such a thing? How could this thing exist inside of me?" It haunted me.

One day when I was in sixth grade, I was doing a paper route—it was my first job—I was riding my bike and throwing the papers and I started crying. I was despairing because of that word in my mind. I couldn't understand how it could happen and how I could be evil. I probably never came so close to wanting to die as then. I couldn't express this internal struggle to anybody. I felt, "I'm the only person who has ever experienced this at such a young age. Everyone else who is young is able to enjoy their childhood. I'm not going to be able to enjoy my childhood fully because there's this ghost of a word which means nothing, yet is there."

I continued to go on retreats with my friend. There was a service every day. At one of them, when I was fifteen, I became completely and totally broken. It was a combination of things—being broken from having the concept of rape in my mind, my mom and the isolation I had experienced at school (I went through a stage of being the smart, nerdy girl).

For the first time, I could visualize Christ on the cross. I could picture God knowing me and seeing my thoughts and knowing that I despised certain things about myself. I could see that Christ saw every aspect of me, everything about my past, everything I didn't like about myself, and that he could forgive me for having that concept in my mind, even though I felt that it wasn't of myself.

The next day I was baptized in the lake, but I was unsure of whether I was a Christian. I had been told that to be a Christian you had to confess with your mouth that Jesus is Lord and that he ascended on the third day. I didn't understand the part about the ascension and being resurrected and why it was so important. The altar call experience I had at the service didn't feel like a conversion. It felt more like an act of repentance, and I felt partly unchanged.

After that retreat, even though I felt uncertain about whether I was actually a Christian, I started reading my Bible. I read Ecclesiastes and came across the words, "When you make a vow to God, do not delay in fulfilling it." That reaffirmed what I had said at the retreat—"I want to follow you. I want to understand this more."

From about that point on, I began to feel less guilt for the thought I had struggled with since fourth grade. When it came back up, I confessed that to God and said, "You see this and I don't know why it is there." So it began to go away. I haven't struggled with it as much since then.

When I was eighteen, I decided to work in a tourist area for the summer. I went partly to start anew in my faith. One day I got out of work early, so I went and hung out in a park. There was a big evangelistic outreach there, though I didn't realize what was occurring at first. It was theatrical evangelism. When I heard them say something about Jesus, I thought, "I really don't need to be hearing this right now," because I had very recently been physically involved with guys. But I decided to move a little bit closer.

A girl came over and sat down. Her name was Emily. She was going to a Bible college near my home. I began talking with her and asking her questions. A few weeks earlier, I had asked a guy I was seeing whether he believed in God and his thought was, "God is a philosophical paradox." To me that was insightful. "Okay, God is a philosophical paradox. It doesn't make sense." And a couple of months before, I had talked with another boyfriend who, along similar lines, had said, "God is very selfish and jealous." So when I met Emily, I had these questions that I felt were valid. "Why is God jealous? He doesn't have a right to be jealous. He is a philosophical paradox. I can't understand how he would allow people to be damned."

Emily listened to my questions. She didn't have answers, but she urged me on with more questions and also presented some answers. Whatever the answers were, they satisfied me enough to convict and encourage me, because I could not be continuing the lifestyle I was in if I was going to be genuinely seeking God. She had grappled with the same issues I had and still trusted and loved God despite unanswered questions. I was in tears that day.

I began to read the Bible more, I began to seek God more. When I went back home, my mom was like, "What happened to you?" I told my story to a friend. I started going to a Bible study. I wanted to understand what it meant to be a Christian.

Then I started going to a church that was very loving, which is what I wanted. But they kept stressing that I needed to be water baptized even though I had already been baptized two years before. I could not understand why my first baptism wasn't enough. Part of me was attracted to the church and part of me felt really wrong. "Something is not right here. Something is very wrong." But I couldn't figure out what it was. I searched the scriptures to see where it said that I had to be water baptized to be saved. But I thought, "I'm such a new Christian, how do I know?"

I met with Emily in a café to talk about it, and everything she was trying to tell me was going in one ear and out the other. Emily felt that she wasn't getting through to me, so she went to the bathroom, where she was crying and praying. While she was there, I was about ready to give it all up. "Forget this. I'm not going to believe anything, because I don't know what to believe." I wanted to believe Emily, but I was ready to become an agnostic again.

While Emily was crying and praying in the bathroom, a guy who was overhearing our conversation came up to me. He was a pastor. He said, "You're saved by faith alone. There's a cult that's on the campuses that is semi-twisting the scriptures. You are not saved by water baptism. You're saved through faith." When he said that, my eyes were completely opened. I thought, "Wow. I can see exactly what he's talking about."

When Emily came back out, I told her what had happened. I was ready to give up my beliefs. I was ready to forget all of it and not believe anybody or anything. But I believed that God was still pursuing me.

It was like the time in a philosophy class that we acted out Plato's cave. Some people went out into the light, and they came back into the classroom to convince the rest of us to go out into the light. All of us in the "cave" had paper bags over our heads. I wanted to stay in the dark, in the cave, so I kept the paper bag over my head. Somebody was telling me, "Stay here," and somebody else was saying, "Come out into the light." I said, "No, I'm going to stay in the darkness." I was determined to stay. But I was torn between the two thoughts. I finally said, "Okay, fine, I'll come out and see the light."

That's kind of how my wanting to become a Christian was. I was being pulled in two different directions—I could stay in one place with guilt, or I could embrace something different.

Kathleen felt a need to be forgiven for the thought that had plagued her since childhood, even though she was not responsible for it. She felt, too, a need to be loved, because she did not receive as much love from her mother as she needed or much attention from her classmates. Reason was not prominent in the experience she had when she was fifteen, though it was present in her conception of Christ as loving her even though he knew about the parts of her that she did not like. Reason became more pronounced later when she started asking questions about God and about what was involved in being a Christian. When she was in the café with Emily, she was ready to become an agnostic again, but when the stranger told her that people are saved through faith, something clicked. No doubt there was a need element in that experience along with a cognitive element, but it is hard to discern exactly what the two are.

6

OBJECTION THREE

Not Everyone Feels Existential Needs

Suppose someone says, "I do not experience any of the thirteen 'needs' you described in chapter two, either as needs, desires or faint longings. I do not feel a need for life beyond the grave or for forgiveness from a divine being. I do, of course, feel a need to be loved, but not by God. And the awe and meaning I feel a need for is not connected to God. Numerous other people do not feel these needs, either. So the existential argument for believing in God does not get started for them or me. It might work for you, but it does not work for me." I shall look briefly at two inadequate responses to this objection before developing a third response.

FEELING A NEED VERSUS HAVING A NEED

It is tempting to respond to the above objection by distinguishing between feeling a need and having a need. That is, one can have a need that one does not feel. Everyone, indeed, has needs that they do not recognize they have. One might, for example, need to embrace the love one is offered without being aware that one needs to do so. Or one might need to express bottled up anger in some appropriate way but not realize that one even has the anger. So it would appear that people can have the need for cosmic security, meaning and forgiveness without being aware of it. And I think that this is so. Many people, believer and unbeliever alike, have existential needs that they are not aware of, just as many people have emotional needs that they are not aware of.

But this phenomenon is irrelevant to the existential argument for believing in God. The second premise in the argument ("faith in God satisfies the needs mentioned in the first premise") would not be true unless one felt those needs. Faith would not satisfy the need for cosmic security unless one felt that one had it. It is the same with the needs to embrace the love one is offered and to express one's anger safely. If one did not feel that one needed to be loved or to express one's anger safely, then performing activities that are designed to satisfy these needs would be useless. Existential needs operate in the same way. Doing something that is supposed to satisfy existential needs would be useless if one did not feel that one had the needs. And, of course, the point of the existential argument for believing in God is to show that faith in God performs a useful function, namely, to satisfy the needs mentioned in the first premise. One must feel the existential needs or the existential argument does not get started. So this first response to the objection of this chapter will not work.

This conclusion means that we need to understand the first premise in the existential argument for believing in God not as saying that we need cosmic security even though we may not feel the need for it, but as saying that we feel the need. We feel the need for awe of God, for a state in which there is pure goodness, for a larger life and for loving God. Unfortunately, putting the premise in this way means that it is much easier to deny. All one has to say is simply, "I do not feel those needs. I do not feel a need to love God or to have a larger life that involves God." It seems, then, that the argument will not work for everyone, as there may well be those who do not feel any of the needs, at least as they are connected to God. But that this is so does not mean that the existential argument does not work for those who do feel the needs; it does (provided it is conjoined with the use of reason in some way). This is the second response to the objection of this chapter. It says that the objection is right, but that the existential argument for believing in God still works, though it is limited to those who feel the needs mentioned in the argument.

SHOULD WE SETTLE FOR AN "IT WORKS FOR YOU BUT NOT FOR ME" APPROACH?

It is tempting to adopt this second response. William James appeared to do so in a somewhat similar context. It is permissible, he thought, for our passional nature to decide between two viewpoints if they cannot be verified by intellectual means alone, provided the question of which viewpoint to adopt is live, momentous and forced.[1] For an option to be "live" to someone, James thought, that person must think that both it and its alternative could be true. If someone does not think that one of the viewpoints could be true, then the question of which viewpoint to adopt is not live for that person. What, then, are we to say if an option is live for one person and not live for someone else? James answers with respect to the religious hypothesis, "If for any of you religion be a hypothesis that cannot, by any living possibility be true, then you need go no farther. I speak to the 'saving remnant' alone."[2] And James goes no further. He does not try to convince those who are not in the "saving remnant" that the religious hypothesis can be live for them.

However, James gives up too quickly. It might be that those who do not regard a particular religion as a living possibility can come to see it as one. This can happen in a number of ways. It can happen if the unconvinced had the key ideas of a particular religion explained to them or if they were told by a practitioner of the religion what it has meant to them to practice it. It can happen if the unconvinced read the religion's sacred writings or the religion's devotional literature, or if they observe the practitioners of the religion close-up. Similarly, those who do not feel any of the needs mentioned in the existential argument can come to feel them. This, too, can happen in a number of ways. One can read descriptions or depictions of the needs. One can observe firsthand people who satisfy the needs with faith in God. One might be brought short by the death of an acquaintance and so be impelled to desire life beyond the grave. Or one might experience awe when hiking in moun-

---

[1]"If we are to discuss the question at all, it must involve a living option." William James, "The Will to Believe," in *The Writings of William James*, ed. John J. McDermott (New York: Modern Library, 1968), p. 732.

[2]Ibid.

tains and be incited to feel awe for something greater.

Furthermore, it might be that those who say they do not feel the needs mentioned in the existential argument for believing in God really do feel them. We should not suppose that people do not feel the needs just because they say they do not or even think they do not. They can be mistaken about what they feel. And they can come to realize that they are mistaken and thus realize that they really do feel the needs.

A third response to the objection of this chapter springs from these possibilities, and it is, I believe, the best response. It is to admit that though some people may not feel the needs stated in the argument, many of these people can come to feel them or become aware that they actually do feel them. This response aims to do two things: first, to make the existential argument for believing in God more convincing to those who do not believe in God, and, second, to make the argument more appealing to those who do. What follows shows how a need to be connected to God can come to be felt by those who do not already feel it and felt more strongly by those who do. By demonstrating that awareness comes in degrees and explaining some of the obstacles to feeling existential needs, the following discussion adds credibility to the existential argument for believing in God. An appendix describes some similarities and differences between this approach and religious psychoanalysis.

DEGREES OF AWARENESS

At any given time, we are fully aware of only a few inner states. What we are aware of can be compared to our visual field. The center of our visual field is focused on what is right in front of us. Off to the sides in roughly a concentric circle around the center is an outer area that we do not see clearly. If we turn our heads and look directly at that outer area, we can see what is in it clearly. We can also become aware of some of what is in the outer area, if, instead of focusing our awareness on what is right in front of us, we focus it on what is in the outer area while still looking at what is in the center. This latter technique involves a bit of a trick, but it can be done.

This analogy to our visual field suggests a way in which we can discover the needs we are only vaguely aware of. It is to look in a certain direction or focus our consciousness on what is in that direction. We cannot, of course, literally turn our heads toward a vaguely felt need, but we can do something like that. We can read or listen to a description or depiction of the need. When we do this, the level of awareness of the need can increase. It is, in fact, likely to increase.

The technique works in several ways. (1) It may provoke a memory of a once conscious experience of the need to be connected to something divine. Reading a description or depiction of the need may bring a memory of that long gone experience to mind, and with it a renewed sense of the need. (2) By giving words to an experience we do not know how to describe, the technique may clarify the experience. In this case, our inability to give words to a felt need is what makes the feeling vague and faint. We do not know exactly what it is. Reading a description of the need makes us say, "So that is what I am feeling," and as a result makes the feeling of the need come to life. (3) The technique can prolong a faint experience, which increases the strength of the experience. In some previous year we might have put a fleeting feeling that we need cosmic security out of mind. A description makes us hold that feeling for more than a mere moment, and as a result it becomes stronger.

These three ways in which the technique of bringing a vaguely felt experience to mind suggest that we have more felt needs than we are consciously aware of. The three ways do not, to be sure, show that everyone feels existential needs, but they do show that more people feel such needs than we or they would initially suppose, albeit unclearly or uncertainly or faintly.

AN EXAMPLE

Let us look at an example of how reading a description of an inner state can bring the feeling of a need to awareness. I shall use C. S. Lewis's description of the longing for heaven in *The Problem of Pain*. He begins by saying that we can be mistaken about the awareness of a desire for heaven: "There have been times when I think we do not desire heaven; but more often I find myself wondering whether, in our heart of hearts, we have ever desired anything else."[3] We do not have a full awareness

---

[3]C. S. Lewis, *The Problem of Pain* (New York: HarperCollins, 2001), p. 149.

of the desire for heaven, and so we think that we do not desire it at all. (I will use Lewis's "desire" instead of my "need.") But the desire may be hidden in a region of our minds that we rarely access. How can we find what is hidden in this unseen region? Lewis realizes that a subtle description is in order. He continues:

> You may have noticed that the books you really love are bound together by a secret thread. You know very well what is the common quality that makes you love them, though you cannot put it into words. . . . Again, you have stood before some landscape, which seems to embody what you have been looking for all your life. . . . Even in your hobbies, has there not always been some secret attraction? . . . Are not all lifelong friendships born at the moment when at last you meet another human being who has some inkling (but faint and uncertain even in the best) of that something which you were born desiring, and which, beneath the flux of other desires and in all the momentary silences between the louder passions, night and day, year by year, from childhood to old age, you are looking for, watching for, listening for?[4]

Lewis is asking us to reflect on everyday experiences—reading a book, gazing at a landscape, engaging in hobbies, acquiring friends—and to notice that in them we are secretly looking for something we cannot describe. The attraction to this something is secret because we are not normally aware of it. And even when we are aware of it, it is only faint and uncertain.

We have never had the something to which we are attracted, Lewis states, but these experiences have given us "tantalizing glimpses, promises never quite fulfilled, echoes that died away just as they caught your ear." How, then, can we know what this desire is? "If it should really become manifest—if there ever came an echo that did not die away but swelled into the sound itself—you would know it."[5] We would know what the something is that we are looking for if it were clearly and distinctly displayed to us, Lewis is saying.

The fascinating feature of this description is that it is intended to provoke into consciousness what is rarely in consciousness, and even

---

[4]Ibid., pp. 149-50.
[5]Ibid., p. 151.

then only in the periphery. If we have had the half-conscious desire for heaven on the occasions Lewis mentions, his description will have a good chance of bringing the desire into fuller consciousness.

The description will have a good chance of doing this if an additional element is added to it, namely, a description of the content of the secret desire for heaven. We might, after all, secretly desire public admiration instead. In looking for books to read, pursuing hobbies and acquiring friends, we might have in the background of our conscious efforts an insistent desire to be admired. We may not know that this is what we desire, as our desire for public admiration may be merely a vague longing. But if we were ever to acquire clear and resounding esteem for our hobbies and friends, we would recognize in it our secret longing. What this alternate possibility shows is that for Lewis's description to provoke an awareness of a desire for heaven instead of an awareness of a desire for public admiration, he has to say something about what the desire for heaven is. Or we must independently have an idea of what it is.

Lewis gives some brief hints of what he regards the desire for heaven to be. He says that it is a desire for an "unattainable ecstasy." It involves being summoned "away from the self." In heaven we will be eternally engaged in giving away to others what we have received. And we will be continually abandoning ourselves to God—opening, unveiling and surrendering ourselves to God.[6] Moreover, we independently know a little of what the desire for heaven is. It is a desire to be free from hardship and struggle, free from the agonies of conscience. It is a desire for inner peace and gladness, for a sense that the terrible pains we have endured will be made up for.

With these ideas in mind, we see that Lewis is asking us to notice what we have not noticed very well—the times when, for a fleeting moment, we have a faint sense of being haunted. We have not known exactly what by, and we have been too preoccupied to try to find out. But when we set aside our preoccupation and focus on the haunting perception, we see that it consists of a faint but nevertheless real de-

---

[6]Ibid., pp. 152, 154, 156.

sire for heaven—not all of heaven, perhaps, but at least some definite feature of it.

OBSTACLES

Unfortunately, there are obstacles to making faint desires come to life. The ones I have mentioned so far are cognitive—faintness of perception, vagueness of perception and shortness of perception. Episodes in which we experience a desire for something divine often lack sufficient intensity, clarity and length for us to recognize them readily. These are intellectual impediments to experiencing the desire, and they can be overcome, to some degree at least, by using cognitive methods, such as reading or listening to descriptions of the desires.

Noncognitive obstacles, however, cannot be overcome just by using cognitive methods. Resistance to existential desires fuels noncognitive obstacles, because the desires have moral and spiritual freight that we do not like. They are not like the desire to recover the memory of an innocent event in the past, which has no moral or spiritual freight attached to it and for which the impediments to remembering are purely intellectual.

We might not like the freight attached to the desire to be connected to something divine for a number of reasons. We might not like having to give up our independence and autonomy if we were to submit to the divine. We might not like having to change our priorities if we became more closely connected to the divine. We might fear the disapproval of others whom we think want nothing to do with the divine. We might not like being wrenched away from the dear self that being in heaven involves, or the sense of littleness we would feel if we were to experience awe of something cosmic.

Noncognitive obstacles to uncovering the vaguely felt desire for something divine operate in this way: We recognize that there is moral and spiritual freight attached to the desire. We do not like that freight. So we do not want the desire. And this makes us blind to the fact that we have it.

The phenomenon of becoming blind because of noncognitive impediments occurs with respect to nonreligious desires and emotions as well. Consider an everyday case of anger. A person who is angry at an accusation that someone has made against her may become blind to the fact that there is some truth to the accusation, because she does not like to think that it may be true. It may take a good deal of conversation with the accuser before she admits its truth.

Anxiety also produces cognitive blindness. We are anxious about our physical appearance, about how others regard us, about our future, about death, and countless other matters. Our anxiety about how others regard us causes us to esteem ourselves more highly than is warranted. We imagine we are heroes who save others from distress or who are admired by all who make our acquaintance. Our anxiety about death causes us to deny it. We will not die, we tell ourselves. Only other people die.

Self-preoccupation distorts our beliefs and cognitive activities in a variety of ways. It skews our perspective and undermines impartiality. It closes us down to new avenues of learning—what is not immediately pertinent to our concerns gets ignored. We are unable to imagine the standpoints of those who believe differently, so we do not truly understand them.

Pride, too, affects our cognitive activities. Because of pride, we engage in unwarranted dogmatism. We disdain beliefs we think are false, we disdain people who have these beliefs, and we become unwilling to listen to them. Our discussions with them become one-way conversations. We do not recognize that we can have strong beliefs and still be gracious to those who differ from us.

If these emotions have these cognitive effects, it is not surprising that they would also produce resistance to having existential desires. The process would work in this way: Anxiety, self-preoccupation and pride cause us to notice that there is freight attached to the desire to be connected to the divine. This freight is that we would have to give up the anxiety, self-preoccupation and pride if we were so connected. We see that having the desire conflicts with having the emotions. We do not like this internal tension, and since we want to hang on to the emotions, sometimes tenaciously, we do not want to have the desire to be connected to the divine or even to know that we have it.

The master analysts of the human condition were aware of the role that resistance plays in acknowledging inner realities. Consider what several of them have said. Søren Kierkegaard makes numerous comments about religious evasion. Here are two: "*Quarrelling with people about what Christianity is* is a mistake, for with very few exceptions their tactics aim at warding off understanding or learning what Christianity is, because they suspect that it is rather easy to grasp, but also that it would interfere with their lives."[7] And, "The most pernicious of all evasions is—hidden in the crowd, to want, as it were, to avoid God's inspection of oneself as a single individual, avoid hearing God's voice as a single individual, as Adam once did when his bad conscience fooled him into thinking that he could hide among the trees."[8] People use a number of tactics to resist knowing what Christianity is or listening to God, Kierkegaard is saying. One of them is to quarrel about what Christianity is. Another is to hide in "the crowd"—a group of like-minded people with which one uncritically identifies so as to abandon one's identity. "Crowd Christians" are those who hide from God by losing themselves in a group of Christians, usually a church. By quarrelling and hiding, one resists knowing that one is not really a Christian. This phenomenon prompted Kierkegaard to declare, "What do I want? Quite simply: I want honesty."[9]

Frederich Nietzsche writes, "A proper physiopsychology has to contend with unconscious resistance in the heart of the investigator."[10] The spiritual world, Nietzsche says, may appear impersonal and devoid of presuppositions, but one who investigates it is blinded by moral prejudices that are unknown to the investigator. These prejudices cause the investigator to resist seeing what is really in the depths of the human psyche.

---

[7] Søren Kierkegaard, *The Diary of Søren Kierkegaard*, ed. Peter Rohde (New York: Carol Publishing, 1990), p. 166.

[8] Søren Kierkegaard, "An Occasional Discourse," in *Upbuilding Discourses in Various Spirits*, trans. Howard V. Hong and Edna H. Hong (Princeton: Princeton University Press, 1993), p. 128. This work is often known as *Purity of Heart Is to Will One Thing*.

[9] Søren Kierkegaard, *Attack upon "Christendom*," trans. Walter Lowrie (Princeton: Princeton University Press, 1944), p. 37.

[10] Frederich Nietzsche, *Beyond Good and Evil*, book 1, section 23, in *Basic Writings of Nietzsche*, trans. Walter Kaufmann (New York: Modern Library, 2000), p. 221.

Sigmund Freud also writes about resistance: "The analysis is faced with the task of removing the resistances which the ego displays against concerning itself with the repressed."[11] What happens when people are undergoing counseling or psychoanalysis, Freud says, is that they resist knowing about desires and patterns of thinking that they find unpalatable. So they resist bringing these desires up during counseling sessions. What the analyst has to do is to try to get the counselee to overcome this resistance so that they can become aware of the desires and thus able to deal with them.

Freud recognizes that resistance to knowing desires is not purely an intellectual matter. "In the end we come to see that we are dealing with what may be called a 'moral' factor, a sense of guilt, which is finding its satisfaction in the illness and refuses to give up the punishment of suffering. . . . This sense of guilt expresses itself only as a resistance to recovery which it is extremely difficult to overcome."[12] The reason the patient does not recover from his neurosis easily is that he resists doing so. But he does not know that he is resisting: "It is also particularly difficult to convince the patient that this motive lies behind his continuing to be ill."[13] His resistance has a moral motive—wanting to avoid the guilt he would experience if he did not continue to punish himself with the suffering involved in the neurosis, or simply wanting to punish himself with the pain of the neurosis. It is this moral motive that produces the patient's blindness to the resistance itself.

Blindness that results from resistance, it is clear, is not simple ignorance, as it is for blindness that results from cognitive obstacles. Cognitive obstacles do not involve resistance to knowing. They can be overcome by engaging in intellectual procedures.[14] But blindness that comes from resistance requires something else to be dissipated: honesty, aware-

---

[11]Sigmund Freud, "The Ego and the Id," section 1, in *The Freud Reader*, ed. Peter Gay (New York: W. W. Norton, 1989), p. 630.

[12]Ibid., section 5, p. 652.

[13]Ibid.

[14]It seems commonly to be assumed that there are purely intellectual issues, and thus purely cognitive obstacles to settling them, but it is not completely obvious that this is so. It may be that every intellectual issue is connected to some emotional or moral one, in which case settling it would involve removing noncognitive obstacles as well as cognitive ones. But the argument of this chapter does not hang on this issue.

ness and willingness. Honesty is needed so that one can admit that they have emotions that conflict with existential desires. Without honesty one will lie to oneself about having the conflicting emotions. Awareness of the conflicting emotions is needed so that one can work on eliminating them. "Uncovering the resistance, however, is the first step towards overcoming it," Freud wrote.[15] If one is unaware of their resistance to being connected to the divine, it will control them. They also need willingness to be honest and aware and willingness to have a desire to be connected to what is divine. Without this willingness, nothing in the process of overcoming noncognitive obstacles will get started.

These points about resistance and blindness explain why some people do not feel the need to be connected to anything divine or do not acknowledge feeling the need. It is because they resist doing so. This explanation is both simple and complex. It is simple because it appeals to one root cause, and it is complex because this root cause is woven throughout one's emotions, desires and inner states. An explanation such as this is needed if we are to make sense of the fact that some people say they do not feel the need to be connected to something divine. In addition, this explanation suggests a way to become aware of the need, namely, to eliminate the resistance to feeling it by becoming honest, aware and willing. My thesis here is that if people are honest, aware and willing, some of them, at least, will become aware of having felt the need. This supports my prior thesis that more people than we would first suppose actually do feel the need. They feel needs of which they are not fully aware.

AROUSING NEEDS

The above discussion about recognizing needs that we are not fully aware of applies also to arousing them. Cognitive techniques can evoke the feeling of a need not previously felt. Perhaps we have never experienced awe before and never thought seriously about it. In reading a description of awe or of an awe-evoking event, such as a childbirth, we might discover that feeling awe is both attractive and important. Or it

---

[15]Sigmund Freud, "An Autobiographical Study," section 4, in *The Freud Reader*, p. 25.

may be that we have never felt much gratitude. Then we read the section in Fyodor Dostoevsky's *Crime and Punishment* in which Raskolnikov is overcome with gratitude because of the unreserved love he receives from Sonya, and he falls to the ground at the haymarket in St. Petersburg and kisses it. After working through Dostoevsky's depiction of the tortuous guilt that Raskolnikov feels, we can hardly help feeling this gratitude.

The same is true for noncognitive obstacles. Eliminating them and the accompanying resistance can open us to feeling existential needs. If, for example, we have an inflated sense of self-importance, we will not be likely to feel a need to be forgiven by God. But if this inflated sense is punctured, we become open to the need and thus are more likely to feel it.

If Freud is right that there is a moral dimension to discovering what is in the unconscious—namely, resistance in the heart of the patient—it seems reasonable to infer that there is the same moral dimension to feeling the needs mentioned in the existential argument for believing in God. Resistance in our hearts must be defused if we are to feel those needs. And when the resistance is defused and the needs are presented clearly, we are more disposed to feel them.

RESISTANCE AND FAITH

It is important to note that the resistance I have been talking about afflicts believer and unbeliever alike. We should not suppose that there is a clear dichotomy between the two, that is, that those who believe in God are free of all resistance to God and that those who do not believe in God are full of such resistance. Faith and resistance are opposed, to be sure, but the human personality can have oppositions within it. And it often does.

Imagine that someone has grown up being heavily criticized by a parent. He accepts it when he is young but later develops sharp resentment toward the offending parent. He harbors a desire to see the parent harmed, perhaps even killed in an accident. His stray thoughts sometimes return to the memory of a hurtful remark. Nearly uncontrollable rage arises on these occasions. At the same time, he is not generally a resentful person and rarely displays any kind of anger. All who come to make his acquaintance know him as an affectionate person. He helps, expresses sympathy, listens and sometimes sacrifices. No one suspects that he possesses seething anger, for he keeps it hidden.

Imagine, also, a married couple. They love each other, are faithful to each other, regularly express affection, and care for each other when they are sick. One of them, however, has recently met someone to whom she immediately feels a connection. She sees him now and then, not by design, but because their circumstances throw them together. She begins to daydream about him, and desires spring up which she dare not admit to her husband. Still, she continues to express love toward her husband in all the ways she has hitherto done.

Those with faith regularly possess these kinds of oppositions. They have desires that do not sit well with their existential desires. They have thoughts that would undermine their faith if they let them. Sometimes they nourish these desires and thoughts. They do this in spite of the fact that they also genuinely want to love God and their neighbors as themselves. They willingly participate in church services and display respected virtues. But even though they sincerely and earnestly do these, they also sometimes desire not to. The best explanation for this phenomenon, I believe, is that those who have faith in God still harbor some resistance to God. Nietzsche's and Freud's concept of resistance, given a religious twist, and Kierkegaard's notion of evasion, afflict people of faith as well as those without faith. People of faith, too, need honesty, awareness and willingness so they can uncover and diffuse the obstructions to faith within them.

AN ANALOGY

My response to the "not everyone" objection can be illustrated by an ordinary psychological case. Let us look at the emotional hermit again, the one who insulates himself from his feelings and emotions. He does not easily reveal them to others, nor does he readily connect to others emotionally. At the same time, he smiles at those he encounters and likes being with them for limited amounts of time. But he does not need extensive love, he says, which is why he lives alone.

One's first response to this scenario might be to distinguish between the need to be loved and feeling the need. The hermit may not feel the need to be loved, one might say, but that does not mean he does not actually need to be loved, for everyone needs to be loved, including him.

This response is no doubt right. But it will not do any good to point it out to him. For he will simply say, "I do not feel that need. Others might feel it, but I do not." It is tempting to accept this reply at face value. But this would be to give up too easily. For there might be things he can do that would cause him to feel the need. He might, for example, read self-help books about loving and being loved. Or he might observe a close-knit family and see how its members give affection to each other. Other people can also do things that would cause him to feel the need to be loved. They can remain steady friends with him and show him special attention on occasion, or they can invite him to events at which other connecting-type persons will be present.

These ways of getting the emotional hermit to feel the need to be loved may encounter obstacles. It may be that his childhood family experiences are preventing him from feeling the need. Perhaps his parents were indifferent and unaffectionate toward him. Or perhaps he has frequently been disappointed when investing himself in friendship or love relationships. In these cases, he may need more than everyday sorts of methods to rekindle the need to be loved, such as counseling. It may even be that he is unwilling to feel the need. In this case, his resistance to it would have to be dissolved before he could begin to feel his need to be loved.

The experience of many people has shown that emotional hermits can come to feel the need to be loved. At the same time, we must respect someone's claim not to be able to feel this need even though they have undertaken the techniques I have mentioned. It is the same with existential needs. The experience of many people has shown that those who have not felt them or who have felt them only vaguely can come to feel them or have them reawakened. But, again, if someone claims not to be able to feel existential needs even after having tried techniques for arousing them, we must respect that claim. Doing so, however, does not undermine either the existential argument for believing in God or the evidential argument based on need, for neither one depends on the assertion that everyone feels existential needs. It is enough that many do for the evidential argument to be convincing. And the existential argument applies to anyone who feels the needs. In the end, William James is right—it is for the "saving remnant," though that remnant is much larger, I believe, than one might originally think.

HARD-WIRED FOR GOD?

Perhaps, one may say, recent evidence that the human brain is hard-wired for God supports the claim that everyone has a need for God. Scientists obtain this evidence by hooking people to machines that are able to detect brain activity when the people are undergoing religious experiences. When they report having those experiences, the machines show that there is extra activity in certain regions of the brain.[16]

For this evidence to support the claim that everyone needs God, it must show that there is brain activity when people feel the need for God. So far, the evidence has not been that specific. It consists largely of showing that there is brain activity when Christians and Buddhists meditate intensely. It does not consist of showing that there is brain activity when people report feeling a need for God or for any of the needs mentioned in the existential argument for believing in God. So as it stands, the evidence does not specifically support the claim that everyone is hard-wired to feel a need for God.

One could, of course, argue that because neuroscience has found brain activity when people report having certain religious experiences, it is likely that there is brain activity when people feel the needs mentioned in the existential argument. Or perhaps neuroscience will advance to the point where it can be much more specific than it currently is, so that it can pinpoint specific places in the brain that become active whenever someone feels a need for cosmic security or a longing for heaven. Would this discovery support the claim that everyone feels a need for God? Unfortunately, it would not. For one of the cognitive or

---

[16]See Andrew Newberg and Eugene D-Aquili, *Why God Won't Go Away: Brain Science and the Biology of Belief* (New York: Ballantine, 2001). Numerous responses to this book's claims can be found online by searching for "hard-wired for God."

noncognitive obstacles to feeling the need may still prevent one from feeling it. Neuroscience might find that there is activity in a different part of the brain that occurs when those obstacles exert themselves. So if neuroscience shows that people are hard-wired to feel a need for God, it would be equally capable of showing that people are hard-wired to erect obstacles to feeling the need. This means that neuroscience is neutral with respect to the issue of whether everyone feels a need for God. The question of whether everyone feels such a need is not answered by finding brain activity when one feels an existential need. It is answered only by inspecting one's own feelings. Neuroscience's findings may all be true, but they would not support the existential argument for believing in God.

Here is an account of need being awakened and reawakened.

MARK: FROM BITTERNESS TO COMPASSION

My parents got divorced when I was two, and I grew up in my dad's house. There was no religion in our house. Other than being baptized in the church, I had never been in church before I was five.

My mom became a Christian when I was five. When I was at her house, she did the motherly thing and put me to bed. Sometimes she stood outside my bedroom and watched me sleep. One night when I was five, after she had been a Christian for about a month, she was standing there, watching me, and as soon as she left the room, I got up, threw off the blanket, and knelt down beside my bed. No one had told me what to do. I had never been to church. I had never had any kind of exposure to God, except maybe for hearing some things from her. She never told me what it meant to be a Christian or to have faith. I did it on my own.

When I was six years old, my mom started getting rare diseases, and the doctors told her she was going to die. It's a strange thing to be six years old, seven years old, and to have to hold your mom in your own arms and not be held in hers because she was too weak to do it herself. It's a strange thing to have to call the ambulance because your mom might be dead when you find her unconscious or going into convulsions. When you're a kid, it seems as if that would be one thing that would deter you from believing in God. But I never got angry at God. I accepted that that's the way things are.

My stepmom didn't like me. She beat me a lot. She tried to break my nose one time by smashing it into a door because I left my pajamas in the bathroom. This was when I was in first grade. The last day she ever touched me was when I was twelve years old. She used almost all the force she had to try to inflict physical damage on me, and it never hurt. I stood up, not a tear, not a wince, not a pain, and looked her straight in the eyes and left. She never touched me again after that. I didn't get angry at God because of that, either.

One night when I was a freshman in college, things got really difficult for me. I had trouble dealing with being alone. I had trouble dealing with not having a church. I had trouble dealing with feeling that I was abandoned by Christians in general. I was dealing with my own imperfection as a human being, with the fact that humans mess up, make mistakes, and that I'm one of them. Some of it was trying to understand what it means to be in a Christian body, trying to understand what it means to be a Christian, trying to understand what it means to have a faith-motivated life.

I went out and jumped into my car and drove all the way to Indiana [from northern Illinois]. This was at midnight. I pulled into a rest area off Highway 65 not too far south of Route 80. I sat on the lawn and didn't run from my pain. I had been doing that all my life. I stayed up all night, wide awake, out in the middle of nowhere on the grass underneath a tree at that rest area.

Finally, the things I was having problems with culminated in one thought. I always thought my faith, what I believed in, had answers. I shouldn't be alone anymore. I shouldn't feel hurt. To me now it seems ridiculous that I would think that. But nonetheless I did. I started to have an epiphany about that. I let myself sit with my pain, which came from wondering why people had hurt me, why I was left alone. I became less afraid to sit in the midst of the pain, in the midst of the fear. I became more comfortable with engaging myself with it and letting the questions roam. I wanted to ask harder questions.

It wasn't a dramatic experience. It was just something I needed to do. I needed to go find a place away from everything else to be entirely alone and experience what it means to hurt and to let it be. I realized that it is a part of life. This is why I still can't get mad at God. I don't understand why we were created in such a way that these particular things occur. But it is that way. As frustrating as that may be to accept, I had to accept it. Imperfection is a part of life, and it comes in the mode of pain sometimes. Understanding that resolved a lot of issues for me.

I started to let go of a lot of things. I stopped being angry at my stepmom. To this day, I'm still not angry at her. What that night in Indiana did was to make me realize that I needed extra compassion on the people who had hurt me. Instead of harboring a lot of anger for them, I started feeling sorry for them.

I was a very bitter person. I had started getting bitter toward my stepmom and my mom and my dad and my stepdad and my church and my friends. I felt betrayed by the whole slew of people who did all those wrong things: a church I had been in for thirteen years that ostracized me; a mom who couldn't really be my mom, because I saw her two days out of the week; a stepmom who was supposed to be the tender, loving parent, who hated me; the dad who was supposed to be there to teach me how to do things, who became apathetic to my existence; a stepdad who didn't understand how to show any emotion except anger and who would take it out on me all the time. I let go of it all and stopped being angry at them.

I've felt like giving up a lot, but there's always that one thing that reminds me of who I am. I'm that five year old kid who, with no prompting, somehow understood it. I don't know how that happened. I won't even begin to explain it and I don't want to. I like that it remains a mystery. I still believe and I'm still that same person.

In some way, Mark knew about faith when he was five. He retained that faith despite severe feelings of rejection and abandonment. During an all-night quest under a tree, he gave up the anger that might have undermined his faith. He saw through the misconceptions that had been causing him so much turmoil. He let himself feel his pain. He also let himself feel his desperate need for tranquility and understanding and freedom from piercing bitterness. These needs sustained his childhood faith.

RELIGIOUS PSYCHOANALYSIS

THE ABOVE DISCUSSION ABOUT UNCOVERING vaguely felt existential needs can be fruitfully connected with what is called *religious psychoanalysis*. In traditional psychoanalysis the analyst seeks to elicit the unconscious influences of the distress that has prompted a person to seek counseling. The idea is that when the counselee knows what is unconsciously influencing her, she will be able to relieve the distress. If she discovers hidden anger toward her parents because of protracted criticism from them as a child, she will know what has caused her current apparently inexplicable aversion to them. And knowing this will help her deal with the anger. The analyst attempts to bring the anger to consciousness partly by asking the counselee questions, partly by making clarifying comments about what the counselee says and partly by encouraging the counselee to describe whatever comes to her mind. This latter technique is called *free association*.

Religious psychoanalysis operates in somewhat the same way. In it, a person attempts to discover hidden motives behind religious behavior. A person who has acted compassionately might ask herself, "Am I doing this compassionate action because I want to show others how religious I am? Do I want to shore up my pride or congratulate myself for being an exemplary Christian?" She would be prompted to ask these questions by her reading, listening or simple reflection. Perhaps something a pastor has said on a Sunday morning has induced her to reflect. Or perhaps she has been reading Søren Kierkegaard, Friedrich Nietzsche or the Old Testament prophets.

Both Kierkegaard and Nietzsche were remarkably good at doing religious psychoanalysis. Kierkegaard tried to uncover the subterranean motives that he thought were causing people in the nineteenth-century Danish church to think that they were Christians when (he believed) they were, in fact, not. His aim was to incite these churchgoers to reflect on what was really going on in their minds so that they could discover their false religiosity and turn from it to true Christian believing.[1] In doing this, he was using religious psychoanalysis as a tool in the service of evangelism. Perhaps this evangelism could be called "back-door evangelism," as it involved slipping in unnoticed rather than making straightforward declarations about what it is to be a true Christian. Kierkegaard himself called his method "indirect."[2] By contrast, Nietzsche tried to uncover the subterranean motives that he thought caused people to adopt Christian virtues so that he could debunk those virtues and with it Christianity itself.[3] Nietzsche's virulent attacks on Christianity stemmed from the unsavory motives he thought he saw behind Christian virtues. If one can set aside Nietzsche's aim while reading his works, they will serve the same function that Kierkegaard wanted his works to serve.

The Old Testament prophets and Jesus, too, engaged in religious psychoanalysis on occasion. Amos declared that those who participated in festivals and solemn assemblies thought they were doing genuinely righteous things, but in reality they were neglecting true righteousness (Amos 5:21–24). Jesus declared that the Pharisees, the really religious people in his day, also thought they had pure motives, when in fact their hidden aim was to justify themselves (Lk 18:9-14).

Trying to discover vaguely felt existential needs is somewhat like the religious psychoanalysis Kierkegaard, Nietzsche, the Old Testament

---

[1] "My whole authorship pertains to Christianity, to the issue: becoming a Christian, with direct and indirect polemical aim at that enormous illusion, Christendom, or the illusion that in such a country all are Christians of sorts." Søren Kierkegaard, *The Point of View for My Work as an Author*, trans. Howard V. Hong and Edna Hong (Princeton: Princeton University Press, 1998), p. 23.

[2] "If it is an illusion that all are Christians—and if there is anything to be done, it must be done indirectly." Kierkegaard, *Point of View*, p. 43.

[3] "What, in all strictness, has really *conquered* the Christian God? . . . Christianity *as a dogma* was destroyed by its own morality." Frederick Nietzsche, *The Genealogy of Morals*, third essay, section 27, in *Basic Writings of Nietzsche*, trans. Walter Kaufmann (New York: Modern Library, 2000), p. 596.

Prophets and Jesus practiced. Both of these attempt to get at feelings we do not know, or only half know, we have. They do so with some of the same techniques. These involve producing triggering conditions—conscious thoughts or feelings that cause one to become aware of hidden thoughts and feelings. In addition, both attempt to discover the emotional, moral and spiritual obstacles to being aware of the hidden feelings. Ideally, religious psychoanalysis results in overcoming such obstacles so that a person can embrace existential needs.

In both traditional psychoanalysis and religious psychoanalysis, however, the motives that are uncovered are negative, whereas the needs mentioned in the existential argument for believing in God are largely positive. The negative motives that religious psychoanalysis uncovers taint the goodness of our virtues—they are not the pure qualities we like to think they are. They also affect our behavior negatively, producing actions that are prideful, lustful and double-minded. The needs mentioned in the existential argument do not taint our virtues or produce unvirtuous behavior. On the contrary, they produce virtuous motives and behavior.

The picture of the human personality that classic Freudian psychoanalysis and Nietzschean religious psychoanalysis gives us is skewed. Because all they seek to uncover are negative emotions and thoughts, the portrait of the unconscious that they present is almost entirely negative. On the basis of their approach, one is apt to assume that the depths of the human personality contain not a shred of goodness. However, if religious psychoanalysis applies also to bringing vaguely felt existential needs to full consciousness (as I suggest), the negative picture is inadequate. As Pascal remarked, we have a "secret instinct, left over from the greatness of our original nature, telling [us] that the only true happiness lies in rest and not in excitement."[4] We may well have a morass of negative motives and emotions buried beneath our conscious awareness, but scattered among them are positive existential desires. These are the ones that both the existential argument for believing in God and the evidential argument based on need rely on. And they are the ones that positive religious psychoanalysis could seek to uncover.

---

[4]Blaise Pascal, *Pensées*, trans. A. J. Krailsheimer (New York: Penguin Books, 1995), #136 (p. 40).

7

OBJECTION FOUR

EXISTENTIAL NEEDS CAN BE SATISFIED WITHOUT FAITH

THE FOURTH OBJECTION TO THE existential argument for believing in God focuses on the second premise of the argument: faith in
God satisfies the needs listed in the first premise. The objection does
not challenge the truth of the premise, but asserts that though it is true
for some people, it is not true for others. Different people satisfy their
needs in different ways. Although some people need faith in God to
satisfy their need for meaning, others find their need for meaning satisfied by pursuing goals without reference to any kind of God. Although
some people find their need to be loved satisfied only by God's love,
others find their need to be loved wholly satisfied with human love.
And although some people find they need faith in the Christian God
to satisfy the existential needs, others find that they can satisfy the
needs with faith in a different God. So the existential argument for
believing in God, or the Christian God, does not work for everyone,
the objection concludes.

Put differently, this objection states that if the argument validates
faith in God for some people, it also validates nonfaith ways of satisfying the existential needs. It does so because the second premise does
not rule out satisfying the needs mentioned in the first premise without
recourse to faith in God or via faith in a non-Christian God. And this
means that the existential argument entails the relativist assertion that

conflicting beliefs are equally valid. If one rejects relativism, as many people do, one should reject the argument that led to it.

What gives this objection its force is that the existential argument is cast in terms of feelings. As we saw in the last chapter, its first premise states that we feel the need to be loved, to possess meaning and so on. So the second premise must state that we feel that faith in God satisfies our felt needs. If it did not say this, there would be no point in having faith, for it would not do what it is meant to do according to the existential argument. The force of the objection comes from the seeming fact that one cannot argue with feelings. One must simply accept them. So one must accept the report of anyone who says that they do not feel that faith in God satisfies their need for love or meaning.

If we could not argue with feelings, this fourth objection to the existential argument for believing in God would indeed undermine it. The existential argument would not work for everyone, and it would entail that relativism is true, which would be intolerable to most people.[1] But, as we also saw in the last chapter, we can argue with feelings. It might be that we are mistaken about them. This is so because our awareness of feelings comes in degrees, which means that we do not see them all clearly. When we make them clearer, we find that we may feel needs that we did not think we feel. We saw in the last chapter, too, that certain obstacles prevent us from feeling the needs mentioned in the existential argument. This means that we can argue with feelings by questioning the intellectual or psychological mechanisms by which we come to have them or by which we are prevented from having them. Last, we saw in dealing with the Tyrant George Objection in chapter five that we can question the value someone places on their feelings. It might be that the value one judges a feeling to have is mistaken.

This chapter develops these points in response to the objection under consideration. First, "the restlessness test" offers a way of trying to discover what best satisfies the needs mentioned in the existential argu-

---

[1]Relativists, of course, would not be concerned about the relativist implication of the existential argument. But neither could they criticize the argument. The person for whom faith in God satisfies existential needs would be as justified in having that faith as would the person for whom nonreligious states satisfy the needs mentioned in the argument.

ment. Second, "the obstacle test" describes some of the barriers that prevent one from feeling that faith in God satisfies the needs. Third, "the value test" proposes a way of ranking the value of our feelings. Last, "the satisfaction test" suggests yet another way of determining whether we are truly satisfied with the means used to satisfy existential needs. All these discussions concede that by itself satisfaction of need is not a sufficient foundation on which to base faith, but they also show how adding reason to satisfaction of need legitimizes the use of need in drawing us to faith. Ultimately the question is, does faith in the Christian God satisfy human existential needs better than any other means?

THE RESTLESSNESS TEST

The restlessness test is designed to determine the efficacy of particular ways in which we try to satisfy the needs mentioned in the existential argument. The test is simply to see whether we are still restless as a result of trying to satisfy them. Let us consider a case to see how it works.

Imagine that someone is restless because they want to be married. They find someone to marry, and the restlessness subsides. But it returns now and then. They have children, and the restlessness subsides more. But it returns again as the children become independent. The person finds new friends and becomes involved with a homeless ministry, and the restlessness diminishes again. Still, it returns in wistful moments when they wonder whether there is something else that they could do, or whether they could develop some new love. They consider loving God, investigate what it means to do so, and then bit by bit come to love God. Their restlessness ceases.

In this case, restlessness drove the person to ever-new loves. Each new love quelled the restlessness some. But it did not quell it completely. There was always the question "Is this all?" nagging the person during fleeting moments. They paid attention to those transient feelings and were finally moved to love God.

Although restlessness sometimes works in this way, sometimes it does not. Some people do not get restless with human love and are not moved to love God. Others get restless even after loving God. Both of these situations actually happen a good deal. So, then, it looks as if the restlessness test may not be reliable.

The thing to say here, I believe, is that although using restlessness as a test of whether our existential needs have been satisfied is not decisive, it can work. Nothing, in fact, is decisive in producing faith. So we must not expect foolproof methods of doing so. Still, restlessness has prompted numerous people to find faith. It has made them feel that some of the ways they try to satisfy their need to love and be loved do not finally do so. These people have become aware of their restlessness, paid attention to it and found the cause of it.

Becoming aware. Sometimes restlessness is easily felt. We are bored with our old loves. We do not know what we really want. We feel unsettled, wondering what would make us feel at ease. On these occasions, we know that we are restless since we feel it acutely. On other occasions, however, our restlessness is not so strongly felt. It hovers in the background of our consciousness. Or it lasts for only a moment and then recedes into unawareness. For the restlessness test to work, we must become fully aware of the boredom and discontent involved in restlessness.

To do this, we may need to become more attuned to what restlessness is, so that we are better able to recognize it when it approaches. Here is how Keith, an engineer in his early fifties, describes his restlessness: "It's been one of the biggest blessings and at the same time one of the biggest curses. There's always been this desire for what's next. It started when I was a little boy. I'd always want to see why I couldn't help my dad or why I couldn't go to work with him; I hoped for the day I could drive a car. It made me get ready for what was coming, what I was wishing for. It would drive me to do things so I could achieve what I wanted. This was the biggest blessing. The biggest curse is that even when I'm having a fairly good time, I find myself thinking, 'What's going to happen next?' And instead of living in the present where I can enjoy life to its fullest, at the moment, I don't always do that. Or I would be assigned a certain task, and I would see somebody else with a different task, and I'd go, 'I want that task instead.'"

Jonathan, a magazine editor in his twenties, says, "Restlessness kicks in when I suddenly feel like I have to find the next step to reach. The feeling of restlessness is that no achievement is satisfying enough." And Kate, in her sixties, says, "Restlessness generally feels uncomfortable, unsettled, uncertain, questioning, 'I know not what,' unfocused, 'jumpy' in mind or body. It's a kind of questing but generally not well directed, with some degree of impatience or confusion. It suggests dissatisfaction with a current state, without knowing what might be better."

Paying attention. We also need to pay attention to our restlessness for the test to work. This is different from being aware of it, for we can be aware of being bored and discontent but not be interested in it, or not ask why, or not be moved to alleviate the discontent in a satisfying way. Paying attention means minding a fact and being engaged with it, willing to do something about it if that is called for. We might, for example, be aware that a homeless person is sleeping in a doorway we are passing, but pay her no attention. If, however, we saw a car barreling toward us as we were about to cross a street, we almost certainly would pay attention to it. In the scenario I described above, the restless person was both aware of his or her restlessness and paid attention to it.

Finding the cause. The person was also aware of what was causing their restlessness. It was that their human loves, good as they were, left them with an empty feeling. It might have been, though, that the person was not able to determine the cause, for restlessness does not come with its cause obviously displayed. This is true for both "afternoon restlessness" and "cosmic restlessness." In the former, we sit and stare, or we get up and do some trivial thing. We do not know what would alleviate our uneasiness. If we could find something that interests us, we would pursue it and our restlessness would cease. But for the moment, on some slow afternoon, nothing interests us. In cosmic restlessness, we may be even more unsure of what is causing our uneasiness, as whole-life considerations are not often in the forefront of our minds. We may not be thinking that we need to be loved when we turn the television on or that we need to find someone to love when we look searchingly at the faces of people whom we pass on the street. We may not be aware of our cosmic insecurity when we put some of our money into a high-interest CD or of our longing for heaven when we look for like-minded people with whom to associate.

To find the cause of our restlessness, we must discover what would dispel it. If it is afternoon restlessness, then pursuing some afternoon project would. If it is cosmic restlessness, then allowing ourselves to be loved by God or believing that God will see to it that we will be in a wonderfully good state after we die would dispel it. Sometimes, though, what we think is afternoon restlessness is really cosmic restlessness. There is, unfortunately, no sure way to discover when this is the case, though this does not mean that we never can.

It is important to note that we cannot assume that the way in which we have alleviated restlessness is defective just because we become restless again. There might be some other cause of the subsequent restlessness. In the scenario I sketched, though the searching person has finally found what she or he has been searching for, no doubt they will become restless again. Daily duties may crowd out their cosmic contentedness. Or they may doubt that they have found what they have been looking for. If the person were to conclude that believing in God did not produce true contentedness, however, he or she would be mistaken. They would not have noticed the intervening conditions that were the real cause of their recurring restlessness.

Although the restlessness test, then, is not always decisive, it has a degree of workability. This fact undermines the presumption on which the objection of this chapter rests, namely, that feelings cannot be challenged. They can be. This means that those who believe that they can best satisfy the existential needs without recourse to faith in God can be mistaken. By using the restlessness test, they may be able to come to feel that faith in God satisfies the needs better than their nonfaith means of doing so.

THE OBSTACLE TEST

The obstacle test is designed to uncover the noncognitive obstacles that prevent one from feeling that faith in God satisfies the needs mentioned in the existential argument. The test consists of looking for desires and motives that are likely to conflict with faith in God.

These obstructing desires and motives are the same as those previously described, which make us blind to existential needs. They do so because they make us averse to the freight attached to the needs. They also make us averse to freight attached to faith in God. Faith requires that we give up our self-preoccupation, our addiction to the "fat, relentless ego."[2] The ego makes us think we are better than others, perhaps even the best in the world. Faith, however, requires humility, which equalizes us. The ego insists on its own way. Faith demands that we yield to others. The ego thinks of itself as autonomous and independent. Faith requires submission to God. The ego demands that other people give attention to it. Faith requires that we give attention to other people. The ego skews moral perception in its favor. Faith does not play favorites in its perceptions. The ego nurses worry and anxiety. Faith lets them go. With faith, we would become persons who regard themselves as equal to others, yield to others, submit to God, give attention, perceive without bias, and let go of worries and anxiety.

Because of the conflicts between faith and the expansive, driving ego, we become blind to the ways in which faith could satisfy the needs mentioned in the existential argument. We do not see that faith in God would give us a larger meaning than that provided by pursuing human goals, or a love that is at least as good as human love. We do not see that, though it is good to delight in human goodness, it is also good to delight in divine goodness.

As with the restlessness test, there is no sure way to discover the blindness that is caused by the nearly irresistible vigor of the ego. But, again, this fact does not mean that nothing can be done to discover the blindness. One can read and listen. One can poke around in one's underground terrain with something akin to what Freud called the "talking cure." The talking cure consisted of telling a therapist whatever came to mind. The idea was that when one did this, one noticed items in one's mind that were connected to what one randomly said. These items were the thoughts and emotions that might have been causing the distress for which the counselee visited the therapist, or, in the current case, blindness and obstacles to faith. By using this method, one might

---

[2]"In the moral life the enemy is the fat relentless ego." Iris Murdoch, *The Sovereignty of Good* (London: Routledge & Kegan Paul, 1970), p. 52. This is not the Freudian ego in contrast to the id and superego but simply the inflated sense of self.

catch a glimpse of brute resistance to faith and goodness, the "No" for which there is no further reason.

There is even less assurance that one can dissolve the resistance. It is so intertwined with our beloved desires and emotions that it is all but impossible to excise. One must, of course, want it gone, and no doubt we do. But, divided as we are, our genuine desire for it to be gone may co-exist with resistance.

Though we cannot ever be certain that we have rid ourselves of resistance to faith and goodness—and the blindness which it fuels—we can achieve assurance to some extent. And this is enough to show that those who do not feel that faith in God satisfies the needs mentioned in the existential argument for believing in God can come to feel that it does.

THE VALUE TEST

In responding to the Tyrant George Objection in chapter five, I argued that it is legitimate to rank the value of the needs mentioned in the existential argument. Additionally, it is legitimate to evaluate the feelings involved in satisfying those needs. The value test ranks the feelings involved in the means used to satisfy the needs. This test rests on the assumption that one will gravitate toward a feeling one judges to have greater value.

If someone declared that hating and terrorizing were ways in which they pursued what I have called a larger life, we would be properly skeptical. In fact, we would roundly reject the possibility. The reason we would do so is that we include moral ideas in the idea of a richer, fuller life. We cannot have such a life if we like to hate and terrorize. Far from being rich, such a life would be mean and constricted. We would say the same about someone who went through their decades bitter at the way they were treated as a child. Forgiving, excruciatingly hard though it is, opens up possibilities that are not available to bitterness. The disposition to forgive makes one receptive to other people's distress. It encourages virtues such as gratitude and trust. It frees one from the tight grip of the demanding ego. Similar points are true about allowing ourselves to be forgiven. When one possesses the disposition to accept forgiveness, one is more open to allowing oneself to be loved. And this promotes more meaningful connections with others, because it eliminates a barrier to those connections.

We commonly rank feelings for their value. And the feelings we acquire are influenced in part by our assessment of their value. If we become convinced that a feeling we currently have has less value than another feeling we could possess, that other feeling has some likelihood of replacing the current one (though this is not a simple matter). So if we become convinced that loving, forgiving and allowing ourselves to be forgiven have more value than hating, bitterness and unwillingness to let ourselves be forgiven, or than simple indifference, then we are likely to want them. And since faith in God includes or is connected to, loving, forgiving and allowing ourselves to be forgiven, we will be more likely to feel that faith in God satisfies our need to engage in these. This means, again, that those who do not feel that faith in God satisfies the needs mentioned in the existential argument for believing in God can evaluate that feeling and use that evaluation to change.

THE SATISFACTION TEST

We can arrive at the same conclusion through employing criteria similar to the need criteria I used in chapter five (in response to the Tyrant George Objection). The point of those criteria was to rule out objectionable "needs" so as to answer the objection that the existential argument for believing in God allows one to believe in a cosmic tyrant who delights in torturing humans. Similar criteria can be used to rank the feelings and emotions involved in the means that are felt to satisfy the needs mentioned in the existential argument. I shall call these criteria the satisfaction criteria and state them in terms of emotions, since emotions satisfy many of the existential needs.

The satisfaction criteria

1. Satisfying emotions are capable of being felt by many others.

2. Satisfying emotions endure.

3. Satisfying emotions are significant.

4. Satisfying emotions are part of a constellation of other satisfying emotions.

5. Satisfying emotions are felt strongly.

We commonly use these criteria, plus an additional one, to determine what emotions satisfy our needs. The additional criterion is,

6. The difficulty of adopting satisfying emotions does not outweigh the contentment it produces.

The central idea is that we need not uncritically accept our emotions but can compare them to other emotions and can ask whether those other emotions would satisfy us better. To use the bitterness example again, we can ask ourselves whether there is some other way of responding to an emotional injury that is not so painful as bitterness. We do this, of course, because bitterness is painful. We want an emotion that reduces or eliminates our pain, that does so for the rest of our lives and that is integrated into the rest of our emotions. Forgiveness, we discover, though involving an anguish of its own, eliminates the sharp pain of bitterness. We feel it as least as strongly as we do bitterness, and it is connected to our other emotions. So we can decide to work toward forgiving one who has mistreated us.

Counselors and therapists also use these criteria to determine which emotions of their counselees will heal them of their distress. The emotions that meet these criteria provide healing from painful memories, the ability to cope with difficult emotions, and control over unruly emotions.[3]

The crucial question now is whether the four tests—the restlessness test, the obstacle test, the value test and the satisfaction test—can show that faith in the Christian God satisfies the needs mentioned in the existential argument for believing in God better than any other means,

---

[3]For example, throughout Irvin D. Yalom's *Love's Executioner and Other Tales of Psychotherapy* (New York: HarperPerennial, 1989), both Yalom and the ten patients whose stories he recounts appeal to the four tests extensively to assess the emotions of the patients (though not explicitly by actually stating the tests). Mihaly Csikszentmihalyi, in his *Flow: The Psychology of Optimal Experience* (New York: HarperPerennial, 1990), uses the four tests (again, not by actually listing them) when describing what he calls "flow": "the positive aspects of human experience— joy, creativity, the process of total involvement with life" (p. xi).

whether involving faith or not. The answer I would like to be able to give is that they can. However, to do so I would have to show two things: (1) that faith in a non-Christian God does not satisfy the needs as well as faith in the Christian God, and (2) that nonfaith means do not satisfy the needs as well as faith in the Christian God. And to show these would require an extensive discussion beyond the scope of this book. Still, a number of observations can be made in support of these two points. First, faith in the Christian God satisfies the existential needs better, much better, in fact, than belief in a cosmic abstract force, as such belief does not address the need to be loved, the need to live after death or very many of the other needs. Second, faith in the Christian God satisfies certain of the existential needs better than belief in most deist conceptions of God, as such belief does not address the need for the close personal connection involved in the needs. Third, faith in the Christian God satisfies at least some of the existential needs better than does the faith or other supreme state in non-Christian religions, such as the Buddhist "emptiness," because the faith in non-Christian religions does not deal with all of the existential needs, such as the need for forgiveness or for life after death in a state free of this life's troubles. Fourth, faith in the Christian God satisfies the existential needs better than non-religious nonfaith ways of satisfying them. For instance, finding meaning through faith in God is better than finding it only through pursuing weekend hobbies. A life of serenity is better than a life of constant and biting anger. Letting oneself be loved by God is better than letting oneself be loved by good, though fallible, humans.

It is important to remember that in all of these observations, "better than" is to be interpreted in terms of the four tests. Faith in God is better than nonfaith means of satisfying the existential needs because it quells our restlessness better, it prompts us to uncover obstacles to satisfaction of the needs better, it has more value, and it is more satisfying, in the ways specified in the tests. It is also important to note that the issue is a matter of degree. This does not mean that nonfaith means of satisfying the existential needs are not "good" at all or that they do not satisfy the existential needs at all. They are good and they do satisfy some of the needs. Human love does, indeed, satisfy the need to love and be loved to a degree. Engaging in worthwhile work satisfies the need to find meaning to an extent. The question is whether nonfaith means of satisfying the existential needs satisfy the needs as well as faith in God satisfies them. My own sentiment is that the four tests show that they do not do so. The tests show, at a minimum, that the emotions involved in satisfying the needs mentioned in the existential argument are capable of being scrutinized and improved. This fact means that the objection of this chapter is blunted, because it assumes that the emotions involved in satisfying the needs must be accepted uncritically. My overall inference is that the four tests move at least modestly toward showing that faith in the Christian God satisfies the thirteen existential needs better than means that do not involve faith in a Christian God. A modest movement, of course, is still a movement.

AN OBJECTION

The advocates of satisfying the existential needs without recourse to faith will reply that the four tests proposed here to support faith in God can be used by them just as legitimately to support their nonfaith means of satisfying the needs. They have found ways of dispelling their restlessness, and they have found this honestly, without being influenced by pride, anxiety or other presumed obstacles to faith in God. They regard their means of satisfying the existential needs as having more value than other ways of satisfying the needs, and they regard these means as meeting the satisfaction criteria. So appealing to the four tests, they will assert, is useless, because nonfaith means are as well supported by the tests as is faith in God.

My response is that, yes, there will be disagreement about how to apply the four tests. There is disagreement about practically every other matter one can think of, in science, law, politics and theology. But this fact does not show that the methods we use in these areas are useless or that one application of them is as good as any other. Some applications of the methods of science and the procedures of lawyerly thinking are better than others. It is the same with applying general evidential criteria, such as empirical adequacy, logical consistency and overall coherence. Some applications of these criteria are better than others, even though people disagree about which ones are better. The argument that faith in God meets the four tests better than nonfaith ways is legitimate, even though others disagree. That is what I have tried to show in this book, but admittedly only to a small degree in the examples I have given. (This is a book more *about* existential reasoning than *in* such reasoning.) The four tests are used in everyday life and employed by psychologists to assess emotions, and these facts speak in favor of using the tests to assess faiths.

The objection does show that we should be cautious in applying the tests. We should not claim that they do more than they actually can. What they can do is give a limited assessment of the ways we try to meet the needs mentioned in the existential argument for believing in God. This fact is important. We are not in a state of undiscriminating chaos, as the objection of this chapter maintains. Though we may not be able to use the four tests to acquire certainty, we are not in a condition of complete uncertainty either.

A CUMULATIVE CASE

Together, the responses to four objections to the existential argument for believing in God make a strong case for the legitimacy of allowing ourselves to be drawn to faith in God by need. They fit the cumulative case strategy that some evidential apologists use in trying to establish the truth of theism or Christianity. The idea in the cumulative case strategy is that evidential arguments strengthen the overall case for Christianity as a group. By itself, each argument has some evidential value, but they reinforce each other because they are connected to each other, so that as a group their evidential value is stronger than the sum of the evidential values of each one. This cumulative evidential value is like that of numerous pieces of evidence at a trial. Each bit of evidence has some value, but when they are conjoined they make a stronger case for conviction or acquittal.[4]

This book's approach fits the cumulative case strategy in three ways. First, there are thirteen needs that faith in God can satisfy and not just two or three. Second, the needs are connected. The satisfaction of one

---

[4]For a brief discussion of cumulative case argumentation, see Richard Swinburne, *The Existence of God*, 2nd ed. (Oxford: Clarendon, 2004), pp. 12-14.

existential need reinforces satisfaction of other existential needs, which increases their drawing power to faith in God. Third, reason can be involved in the satisfaction of existential needs. When need and reason are used together, they reinforce each other. To draw together the argumentation of this book, the ways in which need and reason reinforce each other are stated below with brief comments.

One may come to believe in God by means of evidence or a triggering condition and subsequently be drawn to God by satisfaction of needs. The evidence might be based on the Bible, design in nature, religious experience or even the presence of existential needs in humans. The triggering condition might be any of these as well—it would operate not as a reason in an argument but solely as a cause of believing in God. Believing in God, however, is not simply a matter of believing that something called God exists. It is more like warmly connecting to a person. And for this, satisfaction of need is required—satisfaction of the needs to love and be loved, to have meaning, and other needs mentioned in the existential argument for believing in God. When satisfaction of need is added to evidence, reason-belief turns into warmhearted faith, and when evidence is added to satisfaction of need, one is justified in letting needs draw one to faith in God. Without evidence, satisfying the needs would be indiscriminate. But with it, satisfying the needs with faith in God is warranted.

A special case of conjoining reason and the satisfaction of need in this first way consists of using need both evidentially and existentially. In this case, one believes that the presence of existential needs in humans can best be explained by saying that God made people with those needs, and one is also drawn to faith in God by the satisfaction of them.

There are reasonable criteria to judge the acceptability of needs and desires. That is, criteria exist that tell us which needs and desires can be trusted to lead us to faith and which cannot. These criteria rule out perverse desires and mere wishful thinking, and they also justify us in trusting the satisfaction of legitimate needs.

There are ways of discovering that we feel the needs mentioned in the existential argument for believing in God, ways involving thinking, remembering, clarifying and conceptual probing. Learning what is involved in having the needs is an especially good method of coming to feel them. And something akin to religious psychoanalysis can uncover noncognitive obstacles to feeling the needs.

There are tests by which we can determine whether our faith in the Christian God really does satisfy the needs mentioned in the existential argument for believing in God—the restlessness test, the obstacle test, the value test and the satisfaction test. These tests can also be used to determine whether the nonfaith means we use to satisfy the existential needs really do satisfy us. When we use all of the tests, they have a cumulative force.

The four objections to the existential argument for believing in God are based on the simple satisfaction of need, that is, the mere feeling that faith in God satisfies the needs mentioned in the argument. The point of the objections is that this feeling does not justify such faith. This point is right. But joining reason with satisfaction of need undercuts these objections. It is not just bare satisfaction of need that legitimately draws us to faith in God, but satisfaction of need conjoined with reason in one or more of the ways described above.

The satisfaction of need legitimately draws us to faith in God. This way of coming to faith should take its place alongside the evidential arguments that traditional Catholic and Protestant apologists have used to try to convince people to acquire faith in God.

Here is an account of coming to Christian faith for someone who employed both the restlessness test and the satisfaction test. Neera explains what prompted her to leave the Muslim faith in which she grew up and become a Christian.

(By including this account of conversion from being a Muslim to being a Christian, I mean no disrespect for Islam. Even though Christians and Muslims differ, and even though each believe that they are right, each can respect and welcome the other. It is also worth pointing out that those who grow up in Christian homes sometimes have the same experiences Neera had growing up Muslim.)

From early on, Neera needed to know that she was loved even though she could not measure up to others' expectations. The faith in which she grew up left her with an empty feeling and drove her to investigate other faiths. When, finally, she understood that God loved her, she could not resist accepting that fact emotionally.

NEERA: FINDING WORTH

I grew up Muslim in the Middle East, in the United Arab Emirates, which is a very affluent Middle Eastern country. I come from a particular Shiite sect in Islam. Our conception of faith is that if you do something wrong, you have to do X number of things to wash away your wrong.

That left me with a very empty feeling, which is hard for an eight-, nine-, ten-year-old to understand. It's very easy to ignore it, though, because you're not taught to think about it. You just go through the motions, you do what you're supposed to do, you don't really talk about it. That's not to say that my parents didn't allow me to question my faith. They did, except that they would give me very superficial answers. If I tried to keep at it to really understand, they would pretty much say, "When you're older. You're too young to understand." Or they would say, "You just have to believe this, because this is just what it is."

That's never a very satisfactory answer. It doesn't matter if you're eight or nine, because if you're questioning, that means there's something going on inside you that wants to know. My parents never put me at ease; they never made me feel confident in what I believed. But it was easy not to be too troubled by it because everyone around me was Muslim. I questioned, but not ever to the point where I seriously thought about another faith. That's because of a lack of information. There was no place you could have access to a Bible. I had never seen a Bible until I came to the U.S. I just heard about it secondhand from others.

I came to the States to go to college. That was a very liberating experience, because I started actively to pursue learning about other faiths. My roommate was Hindu, and I went with her to the Hindu Student Council. They talked about different philosophies and different aspects of their faith. I also went to a parachurch organization, InterVarsity. What was interesting to me was that because I grew up Muslim—we are people of the book—I felt I had more in common with Christians. So after a while I stopped going to the Hindu student meetings and went primarily to a church and to the weekly meetings of InterVarsity. It was just to learn, though. A lot of it was intellectual curiosity. "Oh, that's interesting. You believe that? We believe that, too. That's great." I never thought of converting. It was just me learning about other religions.

I started reading the Bible. From that point, a lot of things started to make sense, like, "Does God really love me?" This went back to the time I was seven or eight when I was never secure in the fact that the God I worshipped actually loved me and cared about me. I felt I could never measure up, and I was constantly performing a balancing act. I came to realize that there is a God who knows I can't be perfect and who still loves me, who doesn't put me on a guilt trip of trying to measure up when I know I can't. Growing up, I felt that I couldn't do anything right, and I went through the pain of guilt for years, which paralyzed me.

At 3:00 a.m. one random morning—it was in the middle of May—all of a sudden I got really happy and almost giddy. I couldn't stop laughing. I accepted Christ, actually said the words out loud. Up to that point, I knew what the right decision was, and not just the right decision, but what was right as in true. The faith I was born and raised with was not true, whereas what I had learned about Christ and God and the Holy Spirit was true. But even though I knew that, the problem was that there was no way my family would ever accept that. I am close enough to my family that I don't want to be severed from them, and I don't want to cause them pain. That was a huge block for me. So for about three weeks I cried just about every day. At one point I cried so much I had a really bad headache and had to go throw up. People got really worried about me.

That night in the middle of May I felt a huge burden lifted from me. I felt I could face my family and still be happy, still know that I was doing the right thing, even though I could see pain in my future. In that moment, this was the right thing to do. It was a force compelling me to do it. I felt that I could not *not* do it. I didn't think about the "What if I don't do it?" part. There were no two ways about it.

It's complicated by the fact that I was abused from the time I was twelve to before I left for college. The feelings I struggled with most at the time of the abuse were loathing myself and feeling dirty, which culturally for me was very difficult. I come from a very shame-based culture. It breaks you down, because it makes you feel worthless, even though what happened to you is not something you caused. Somehow you feel as if you brought it upon yourself, even though you were twelve and couldn't do anything about it.

In that moment in May, I had the feeling of being loved and the feeling that God wasn't wagging his finger at me and going, "Naughty, naughty. Tsk, tsk." I felt that God was walking alongside me, as opposed to being above me judging me or squashing me. I felt that God was helping me with the feelings that had surfaced as a result of the abuse. I had never talked about it to anyone before I went to college. So when I first talked about it, it was as if a dam burst, and I questioned pretty much everything in my life up to that point.

The feelings didn't go away right away when I accepted Christ. I still struggled with them. What I've become attuned to is the lie that I am not worthy. Even though there are times that I break down and say out loud that I am not worthy, that I am unclean or that it's my fault, inside I know that it is not true. It's still a reflex mechanism that I have. I explode and say, "Fine. I'll never be good enough. I'll curl back into my shell." But more and more I know inside that I'm just saying the words and don't really believe them.

What keeps me going is that I look at Christ's life and the

people he chose to associate with. That's how I know I am not any less worthy than anybody else—because if God can condescend to be with Mary Magdalene, who knowingly did wrong things, then God can love me, because I did not knowingly do those things.

8

FAITH AND EMOTION

"Some people think faith in God is a feeling, an emotion, a comforting sentiment, a druggy buzz into which one escapes to avoid reality. But Father Gilman advocated and demonstrated that Christians are supposed to be reality-oriented. We aren't supposed to escape life with its occasional sorrows and sufferings."[1] So writes one Christopher Bowhay in honor of Richard Gilman, an Episcopalian priest who served a tiny mission in Marin County, California, and who became a mentor to Bohay, who was then a seminary student. These words represent a conception of faith and emotion held by many Christians, theologians and philosophers. According to this conception, faith is not feelings or emotions, for these are fickle and shallow; they entice us to be self-absorbed, sweep over us unannounced and are substitutes for action. Faith, however, should be stable and enduring, in our control, out-going instead of self-centering and should spur us to action.

As we have seen from the faith journeys described in this book, faith often appears to consist of both belief and emotion. Both play a role in the following accounts, though the first account seems to have more emotion than the second. Candace is a former minister in her fifties. William is in his twenties and is currently re-evaluating the Christian faith he grew up with.

---

[1]Christopher Bowhay, in *To Honor a Teacher: Students Pay Tribute to Their Most Influential Mentors,* coll. Jeff Spoden (Kansas City: Andrews McMeel Publishing, 1999), p. 66.

CANDACE

When I first knew God, I called her Gramma God. It was a life-changing experience. It became a connection inside me with God. When I care for that connection, I find courage to live and to show the world that the connection is there. That connection is strong when I can get myself out of the way and let God act through me.

I've had so many experiences of God caring for me that I know when she's there with me. When I go away from God and do things that aren't of God, she's there waiting. When I come back to God, it's a comfortableness. It's a rightness inside of me.

Naming God is important to me. When I am in a worship service and God is named by the presiding person at the service, not with traditional male language but with female language, she's there and I'm meeting her, and I greet her there. Colleen Fulmer's music names God in this way, and so does Kathryn Christian's song "Come, Holy Mother." I reach out to that.

I love the connection with God. I get hungry for it. If I have not seen my children and grandchildren in a month, I get hungry for the sight of them. My eyes need to see them, and I need to hug them. The phone won't do. It is the same with God—the center of me needs to touch base with the center of God herself.

WILLIAM

If there is a God out there, an ultimate purpose or something that we were manufactured for, the purpose of all our being, it would have to make sense, at least enough for me to believe in it. I can't accept something if it seems counterintuitive. I operate predominantly on the intellectual level, maybe not predominantly, but I like to think I do. If something is not logical, then I can't accept it.

I want to find meaning for my existence and a way to be more fully realized as a person, to be a better person. Part of that for me

> is having a sense of security and having a sense of acceptance
> and love. I find it is really hard to be in relationship with people
> and feel that you are completely accepted or loved in spite of
> everything. That's a big need for me going into faith.

Faith, for it to be genuine, should consist partly of emotions. Arguing for this requires rescuing emotions from the disrepute Bowhay's dismissal of them represents. It also requires a picture of faith that is hospitable to emotion. Because faith in God consists partly of satisfaction of need, and because satisfaction of need is an emotion, faith in God consists partly of emotions. This view invites fruitful comparison to the views of Aquinas and Kierkegaard.

CRITIQUES OF EMOTION

A number of critiques have been leveled against emotion. The discussion below begins with the one most often mentioned.

Emotions change. Emotions cannot be what faith consists of, says this first objection, because they are too capricious and flighty. They change often, sometimes daily or hourly. Faith, however, is stable. It does not change from day to day but remains the same.

Immanuel Kant, an eighteenth-century German philosopher, makes the classic case against feelings and emotions, though in a moral context. Inclinations, Kant says, are much too unstable to serve as motives for doing what is good. "Inclinations vary; they grow with the indulgence we allow them, and they leave behind a greater void than the one we intended to fill. They are consequently always burdensome to a rational being, and, though he cannot put them aside, they nevertheless elicit from him the wish to be free of them."[2] It does not matter that inclinations are good, Kant says; they cannot be relied on. "Even," he continues, "the feeling of sympathy and warmhearted fellow-feeling . . . is burdensome . . . to right-thinking persons."[3] It is duty that should

---

[2]Immanuel Kant, *Critique of Practical Reason*, trans. Lewis White Beck (New York: Liberal Arts Press, 1956), p. 122.
[3]Ibid., p. 123.

motivate us—the moral law, given to us by reason—for it is not subject to the vagaries of inclination. By extension (though Kant does not make this inference), faith cannot consist of inclination, desire or emotion, for these are much too changeable.

From less philosophical sources, one hears the same criticism. Ministers admonish us not to trust our feelings, because they come and go. Writers on Christian spirituality advise us how to maintain our faith through despair and depression. We need to base our faith on God, who never changes, not on unreliable feelings, they say. In these criticisms, theoretical and popular, emotion is said to be defective and untrustworthy because it fluctuates so much. What is needed for the moral life and faith is something far more steady and unwavering.[4]

There clearly is truth to this critique of emotion. Emotions change. And they can undermine faith when they do. But there are two responses to the critique. First, whatever replaces emotions in our conception of faith (or of the proper moral motive) is also subject to change; and second, emotions can be just as stable as faith is supposed to be.

No matter what faith is said to consist of instead of emotion, it can change just as much as emotion. Faith is often said to consist of commitment. But commitment wavers. It comes and goes as much as emotions do. So according to the critique, faith could not be commitment. Nor could it be assent based on reason, that is, believing true things about God. For this, too, varies as doubts assail the believer and as daily desires cause beliefs to wane. If, then, change were a reason for rejecting emotion as a component of faith, there could be no faith.

An advocate of the critique might reply by saying that commitment is based on God, who does not change, and that true beliefs are based on facts, which also do not change. But this reply misses the point. The question is what faith *consists* of, and faith does not consist of God or of facts. If the commitment or assent conception of faith were correct, faith would consist of commitment to God or beliefs about God. And these can change even though God and the facts do not.

Moreover, emotions can be stable and enduring. Certainly some are

---

[4] I have not distinguished between inclinations, desires, feelings and emotions because doing so does not matter for the purpose of this first critique.

not, as the critique rightly maintains. But others are. Think of the trust that develops between two longstanding friends or between people who are married to each other for decades. Think of the fear an acquaintance has toward large dogs because of an unpleasant experience with one as a child. Countless emotions have remained constant more than they have fluctuated. The proper reaction to emotions that change is not to excise them (unless, of course, they are undesirable), but to develop steady emotions, ones that are sturdy enough for faith to consist of. Though trust in God wavers, we do not regard this fact as a reason for rejecting trust as a component of faith. We say that it can be maintained at a reliably even level even though it sometimes varies. So here is the first thing to be said about faith as an emotion: faith is a minimally changing, enduring and stable emotion.

Emotions are short-lived bursts of high-pitched passion. The second critique of emotion is connected to the first. Emotions are conceived of as both short-lasting and high-energy occurrences. One suddenly has them, is exhilarated or distressed for a moment, and then is calm again. One is ablaze with love for God or has fervent concern for the plight of the poor, then goes about one's normal business without the blaze or fervent concern. Faith, however, is neither short-lived nor high-pitched. It remains after the blaze has subsided. We cannot, in fact, maintain high-pitched passion for long. We must have calm. True faith is that calm. It is constant concern instead of brief explosions of feeling.

This critique is right in saying that we experience some emotions as intense and for a short time. Grief is one such emotion. If someone we dearly love dies, we are likely to be overwhelmed by bitter episodes of grief that wash over us. We will feel sorrow at a level that consumes our attention and emotional energy. But our grief can also be a less intense daily sorrowing. In fact, grief often lasts beyond the initial, explosive feelings. Though those initial feelings come back to us on occasion, most of the time grief is not nearly so strong. We cannot, in any case, hold such a burning sensation for long, as the critique rightly asserts. But we can grieve over long periods of time.

Repentance is another emotion that we can have at different levels of intensity. Like grief, our first experience of repentance may be sharp and cutting, as it was for Allen in chapter three. But other experiences of repentance may be much less piercing than the first one. They can be daily sorrowings.

The daily sorrowings of grief and repentance are genuine emotions. It is simply not legitimate to maintain that the real emotions are the initial bursts of high-pitched passions and that the daily sorrowings are not emotions. The daily sorrowings are just as much emotions as the initial bursts. We feel them, they are ways of reacting to events, and they involve interpretations of those events—all of which characterize emotions, though without the sharpness.

So, then, faith, too, can be a long-lasting, evenhanded emotion. It can remain stable through the comings and goings of high-pitched passions that may undermine it. The critique misconceives emotions.

This conclusion should not be taken to mean that faith is never passionate or earnest. It certainly can be. However, the earnestness could not be sustained continuously, that is, felt at a high level for much more than a few moments. But it would reappear from time to time. And in between these high-pitched episodes, it would still be faith. A passionate faith is both high-pitched and calm—high-pitched for brief moments and calm for sustained periods, in the same way that grief and repentance vary in intensity from time to time. Faith would still be the same emotion through its variations of intensity, just as love for a person is the same even though it is exhibited enthusiastically on some occasions and calmly on others.

Emotions are disruptive. Emotions are often thought of as wild and disruptive. They undermine the moral ideals to which we have committed ourselves. They sidetrack us from our goals and plans. They "make us do things that, with just a moment's clear thinking, we certainly would not do."[5] They are like wild animals that dash off on uncharted paths.

Plato pictured emotions and desires as one of two horses that pull a chariot. The other horse represents what is noble and good in the soul of a person. The charioteer tries to manage the two horses but finds it

---

[5]Robert C. Solomon, *True to Our Feelings: What Our Emotions Are Really Telling Us* (New York: Oxford University Press, 2007), p. 3. This is not Solomon's own view.

difficult to do so because the horse representing desires and emotions is wild and unruly. Its unruliness often prevents the charioteer from guiding the chariot in the right direction.[6] If emotions were as wild as this conception pictures them to be, faith in God would not be an emotion. At least it would not be what we conceive faith should be.

As with the previous critiques, this one says something right about emotions and desires. They are sometimes wild and disruptive, and when they are, they can lead faith astray. A passion for enhancing one's reputation or an attack of anxiety can do this. Just as often, however, emotions sustain faith. Think of tranquility. In tranquility, one's composure is peaceful and serene. No wild passion or anxiety afflicts one. No turgid emotions sway one this way and that. One sees life as worthwhile: it is good to work, good to play, good to give and good to appreciate moral beauty in others. This kind of emotion could easily contribute to faith in God instead of undercutting it.

A high-energy emotion can also contribute to faith. Not all high-energy emotions are like wild horses that charge off in every direction at once. Some have a clear direction. Grief and repentance are like this, and both can contribute to faith. Grief can lead one to think of the brevity of life and of meaning and, from there, to conceive of faith in God as the only true source of meaning. Repentance can lead one to trust in God as a forgiving being who frees one from addiction to sins.

If emotions are not always wild and disruptive, then not only can they contribute to faith, but faith can actually be an emotion. It would not be an unruly, stormy, blustery and undisciplined emotion that takes us in the wrong direction, but would be more like trust in a faithful and loving person.

The trouble with the last two critiques of emotion is that they use the wrong paradigm of emotions. They take the more noticeable ones, because they are so intense and disruptive, as representative of all emotions. However, a little looking at the extensive array of emotions shows that numerous other emotions are not as intense or disruptive. The next critique commits the same fallacy.

---

[6]Plato *Phaedrus* 246A-E and 253C-254E. See also *The Republic* 439C-441E, for a similar description but without the chariot analogy.

Emotions happen to us. This critique says that we do not have control over whether we have emotions. We are not active initiators of them, because they come to us unbidden, sometimes with high-pitched passion. But we do have control over whether we have faith. We initiate and are responsible for faith. So it cannot be an emotion.

My response to this critique is twofold: faith sometimes comes to us in the way this critique says emotions come to us, and we have more control over emotions than the critique allows for.

Faith sometimes grows on us without our actively choosing it. Someone who regularly associates with people of faith may find herself acquiring that faith. It rubs off onto her in the same way that the mannerisms of intimate friends rub off onto each other. Or faith can arise spontaneously in response to some circumstance, just as compassion can arise instinctively in someone who reads the life story of a homeless person in a city newspaper. The same can happen when reading a novel or watching a movie. If the main character has traits that one wants to emulate, the depiction of those traits provokes one, almost without thinking, to adopt them.

Those who say that faith must always be chosen have a wrong psychology of how faith operates. It often operates as love does. Love is sometimes a nearly involuntary response to someone's kindness or to the attention they give. Love often grows simply by two people being together or by their acting in loving ways, such as by giving simple acts of affection. The acts are both products of love and the creators of love. They work in the way spoken expressions of gratitude work in little children. A parent says to their child, "Say 'thank you.'" The child does, with little or no sense of gratitude at first; however, as instances in which the words multiply, so does the child's gratitude.

The acquisition of trust in God often comes about in similar ways. Observing others whom we believe trust God can cause us to trust, without our being aware that this is happening. Reading the Bible and learning about God can also produce trust, as can feeling that God is present to us. So can acting as if we trust God or believing as if we trust God. The "as if" believing can produce actual trust, just as acting as if we love someone can produce actual love.

If we acquire faith in the way we are said in this critique to acquire emotions, then faith can be an emotion. It is no objection to faith's being an emotion to say that we acquire emotions passively, for we sometimes acquire faith passively.

It would, however, be an objection to regarding faith as an emotion if we were entirely passive in acquiring emotions. For we have some control over whether we acquire faith. In fact, we have a good deal of control. But we also have control over whether or not we acquire emotions. We are not entirely passive with regard to them. We sometimes actively initiate them.

Consider grief again. Though it is obvious that grief often comes to us without our inviting it, we can also call it up. Suppose I haven't thought of Peter, who was killed in a fiery car crash more than a decade ago, for some time. I regard it as appropriate to his memory to grieve his death on occasion. So I get out my favorite photo of him, the one of him and me and a mutual friend. I look at it with fondness, remembering good times we had together. And I grieve.[7]

Or suppose someone likes to nurse a particular anger. It came to her spontaneously when she was falsely accused of lying. Later, because she dislikes the person who accused her, she wants to recall the anger. So she thinks of the situation in which the accusation occurred, and the anger returns. The person savors it, feeling its deliciousness.

Notice that in neither of these cases is the engendered emotion a product only of choice. It is, in fact, pretty nearly a psychological impossibility to produce an emotion simply by choosing to have it. There is always some intervening step—looking at the photo of Peter, thinking of the accusation. What we are choosing to do is to produce the emotion by means of these intervening steps. As Robert Solomon put it, "You cannot 'simply' decide to have an emotion. You can, however, decide to do any number of things . . . that will bring about the emotion."[8] This means that though we do not have direct control over

---

[7]Peter Lu, a former student, was killed in a fiery car crash in 1997 on his way to see his mother, who had flown from China and had waited in Chicago's O'Hare airport six hours before learning of Peter's death.

[8]Solomon, *True to Our Feelings*, p. 197.

producing emotions, we have indirect control. But indirect control is still control.

The chief means by which we control our emotions is through attention.[9] Our attention consists of what our minds are consciously thinking of, which we can control. Although thoughts and feelings race through our minds most of the time, we can interrupt this "stream of consciousness," to use William James's phrase, and call to mind a new thought. Doing so can play a role in bringing about trust in God. We can think of individuals or activities that will produce it, such as people who display trust. Although trust sometimes comes to us unsought, we can cultivate it and make it into our abiding stance toward God. So if faith in God consists of trust, it will not always just happen to us.

Emotions are blind. This critique asserts that emotions contain no cognitive component. They are raw feelings that are blind to matters of truth or falsity. They are like impetuous anger that vents itself on the first person who happens along or dumb love that does not discriminate between worthy and unworthy objects.

Faith, however, is not blind. It can apprehend a worthy object for itself and can recognize what is true or false. So faith cannot be an emotion, the argument goes. Nor can faith be part reason and part emotion, because then it would be at war with itself, like Plato's two horses pulling a chariot in different directions.

The antagonism between faith and emotion has often been a major theme in Christian thought. C. S. Lewis is a representative example. Faith, he says, has two senses. "In the first sense it means simply belief—accepting or regarding as true the doctrines of Christianity." Lewis's answer to the question of what undermines faith is that "it is not reason that is taking away my faith: on the contrary, my faith is based on reason. It is my imagination and emotions. The battle is between faith and reason on the one side and emotion and imagination on the other." What happens to a person who is struggling with his faith is that "all at once his emotions will rise up and carry out a sort of blitz

---

[9]"The key means of control is the human ability to freely deploy attention." Sidney Callahan, *In Good Conscience: Reason and Emotion in Moral Decision Making* (New York: HarperSanFrancisco, 1991), p. 112.

on his belief."[10] Faith, then, according to Lewis, "is the art of holding on to things your reason has once accepted, in spite of your changing moods."[11] Michael Paul Gallagher, in the *New Westminster Dictionary of Christian Spirituality,* mirrors this last statement: "Faith means being able to survive one's moods."[12]

This account of the conflict between reason and emotion contains all of the previous misconceptions of emotions, plus a new one. Emotions come and go, but reason remains stable. They are short bursts of high-energy feeling. They disrupt reason instead of contributing to it. We are passive regarding emotions—all at once they rise up and threaten to overpower reason. And, the new one, they are blind to the truth; it is the job of reason to know what is true. On this account, emotions are untrustworthy, certainly not deserving of constituting faith.

Emotions fare much better, however, in Lewis's second sense of faith. Faith in this sense is "the change from being confident about our own efforts to the state in which we despair of doing anything for ourselves and leave it to God." In this change, one "puts all his trust in Christ."[13] Emotions are involved in this change—despair (of a good kind) and trust, among others. If this distrust of oneself and trust in Christ are to constitute faith, they must remain stable, they cannot simply be bursts of passion, they cannot be disruptive, we must have some control over them, and they cannot be blind.

I want to pursue this last thought—that emotions are not blind. What I will do is make a case for the thesis that they are imbued with reason. The critique is right—if emotions were blind, they would not be suitable for faith. But as they are not simply "raw feels" that are devoid of reason, they are suitable for faith.

Conceiving of emotions as consisting partially of reason has become increasingly prominent among psychologists, philosophers and an oc-

---

[10]C. S. Lewis, *Mere Christianity* (New York: HarperCollins, 2001), pp. 138, 139, 140.

[11]Ibid., p. 140. Lewis does not distinguish between emotions and moods, though that is not important for his purpose.

[12]Michael Paul Gallagher, "Faith," in *New Westminster Dictionary of Christian Spirituality* (Louisville: Westminster John Knox, 2005), p. 298. I am ignoring differences there might be between emotions and moods, as neither Lewis nor Gallagher make a distinction between the two.

[13]Lewis, *Mere Christianity,* pp. 146, 147.

casional theologian during the last half century. In 1962 two psychologists did an experiment in which they injected people with a drug that caused a certain physiological sensation in them. They found that the subjects could not identify the sensation as a particular emotion unless there was a cognitive context for the sensation. They also found that when the cognitive context was varied, the subjects reported experiencing different emotions. The psychologists concluded that an emotion is "a joint function of a state of physiological arousal and an appropriate cognition."[14] Philosopher Martha Nussbaum, in her monumental *Upheavals of Thought: The Intelligence of Emotions,* argues that emotions "involve judgments about important things, judgments in which, appraising an external object as salient for our own well-being, we acknowledge our own neediness and incompleteness before parts of the world that we do not fully control."[15] They are not just "'non-reasoning movements,' unthinking energies that simply push the person around, without being hooked up to the ways in which she perceives or thinks about the world."[16] To support her thesis, Nussbaum gives an extensive analysis of the judgments involved in compassion. Compassion involves the judgment that the suffering of someone is serious, that the suffering is not caused by the sufferer's culpable action, and that it is a significant part of one's own scheme of goals and ends. The emotion of compassion consists of these judgments along with concern for the sufferer's plight.[17] Theologian Matthew Elliott, in his *Faithful Feelings: Rethinking Emotion in the New Testament,* argues for a cognitive conception of emotion. "Emotions," he writes, "are not primitive impulses to be controlled or ignored, but cognitive judgments or construals that tell us about ourselves and our world."[18] This view of emotions, he asserts, is

---

[14]Stanley Schachter and Jerome E. Singer, "Cognitive, Social, and Physiological Determinants of Emotional State," *Psychological Review,* 69 (1962): 379-99, in *What Is an Emotion? Classic and Contemporary Readings,* 2nd ed., ed. Robert C. Solomon (New York: Oxford University Press, 2003), p. 113.

[15]Martha C. Nussbaum, *Upheavals of Thought: The Intelligence of Emotions* (Cambridge: Cambridge University Press, 2001), p. 19.

[16]Ibid., pp. 24-25.

[17]Nussbaum, "The Cognitive Structure of Compassion," in *Upheavals of Thought,* pp. 304-27.

[18]Matthew A. Elliott, *Faithful Feelings: Rethinking Emotion in the New Testament* (Grand Rapids: Kregel, 2006), p. 54.

embodied in the New Testament's references to emotions: "It is clear that the New Testament authors generally write about emotion from a cognitive perspective."[19]

What, then, is the cognitive component of an emotion? It is, I believe, a construal.[20] A construal is a way of seeing something. Suppose I am on a farm where groundhogs abound. One day I step out the front door and spot what looks like a small, upright log in the tall grass in front of the barn. I am puzzled at that, as there was no log there yesterday. So I go to investigate. Suddenly the log moves and runs off. What I first construed as a small log turns out to be a groundhog. When the "log" moves, I immediately change my construal. At first what I saw as a brown, stationary piece of wood, I now see as a furry animal.

Now let's consider a similar case in which emotion is involved. Suppose I hear that an acquaintance has lost his wallet with all his identification and credit cards, including his passport. I immediately have pity on him (but not compassion, as compassion requires a desire to help relieve the suffering of the sufferer, and I can do nothing to help him). The next day, though, when I express sympathy to my acquaintance I learn that it was only a library card that he lost, which can be easily replaced. My construal of his situation changes, and my sympathy lessens considerably or disappears entirely.

In this second case, the emotion I had toward my acquaintance depends on my construal of what has happened to him. This construal consists of two elements. The first is a cognitive apprehension of my acquaintance's situation—he has lost something and is (I suppose at first) feeling a good deal of distress. Later, when my perception of his situation changes, my emotion does as well. The second element of the construal is an assessment of the situation in which my acquaintance finds himself. A mere factual belief about his situation is not enough to constitute the construal, as it is with the log and the groundhog. I must assess my acquaintance's loss and subsequent distress, that is, regard

---

[19]Ibid., p. 238.
[20]I am following the terminology of Robert C. Roberts in his *Emotions: An Essay in Aid of Moral Psychology* (Cambridge: Cambridge University Press, 2003). Emotions, he says, are "concern-based construals" (p. 64).

them as desirable or undesirable. Otherwise, I would have no pity or any other emotion. When I learn that he has lost only a library card, my assessment of the severity of his situation changes, and with it the pity I had at first.

These two elements of a construal are present in many, perhaps nearly all, of our emotions. Suppose I hear that someone has said something unkind about me. I immediately get angry. Later, when I learn that she did not say what I think she did, my perception of her changes and my anger dissolves. In this case, my anger depends on my perception of what happened and my assessment of its undesirability. When my apprehension of what happened changes, so does my assessment, and the emotion I first had leaves.

Trust works in the same way. When I trust someone, I must perceive that person to be reliable. Reliability is not enough, though, for I might not want to trust someone who is reliable. I must also perceive him to be worthy of trust—this is an assessment of the person's character. If I were to discover that the person is not reliable or were to change my mind about the worth of his character, I would withdraw my trust.

The construals in these emotions are cognitive because their elements are cognitive. The apprehension of the object of emotion is cognitive, as it contains concepts about the object. The assessment is as well, because it, too, involves having concepts. So the emotions are not blind feelings, devoid of conceptual content.

Most of the time these construals are not explicitly conscious—I do not consciously formulate my perception of the person who has offended me or the assessment of their offense in a declarative statement. This is the reason I have used "apprehension," "perception" and "assessment" instead of "belief" and "judgment" in describing construals. Beliefs and judgments are normally thought of as conscious mental states, whereas construals are rarely fully conscious. And beliefs and judgments can normally be articulated in declarative sentences, whereas construals are more like unarticulated perceptions. Something may, nonetheless, jog us into thinking about an emotion, in which case we might become aware of the construal and formulate what we perceive the object of the emotion to be. In this case, the emotion would contain an explicit belief or judgment.[21]

Some of our emotions are, to be sure, more like blind feelings that are devoid or nearly devoid of the conceptual content in a construal, such as raw rage which strikes out at others indiscriminately. Most emotions, however, are not like raw rage. They involve attending to objects and making assessments. They are not pitted against reason, but operate in conjunction with reason.

My point is not that emotions contain two separate parts, a feeling and a cognition, but that these two features are fused into an indissoluble unity. The feeling that constitutes an emotion itself construes objects in certain ways. The feeling is as much a construal as it is a feeling. As Mark Wynn put it, "feelings themselves may be the bearers of understanding."[22] There is a spectrum here. At one end, pure thought apprehends its objects without feeling. At the other, pure feeling has no conceptual content. In the middle, the two are joined into one. In these joinings, to use Wynn's words, "concepts and primal responsiveness are fused so as to produce a unified, affectively toned perception."[23] That is, thoughts and feelings join to produce what can be called an *emotionally-toned construal*.

An example of an emotionally-toned construal is an experience of God's presence. A feeling is fused with the thought that God is present to us. The feeling may be one of soothing comfort, or it may be one of overpowering awe. But it is not blind comfort or awe, that is, unknowing sensation. For the feeling knows its object. It knows that the object of its comfort or awe is God. As Wynn put it, "God's presence may be registered directly in our felt responses (rather than being apprehended in some other fashion, which in turn engenders a felt response)."[24]

---

[21]Robert C. Roberts makes the distinction between construals and judgments in *Spiritual Emotions: A Psychology of Christian Virtues* (Grand Rapids: Eerdmans, 2007), pp. 11, 24.

[22]Mark R. Wynn, *Emotional Experience and Religious Understanding: Integrating Perception, Conception and Feeling* (Cambridge: Cambridge University Press, 2005), p. 91. See also pp. 90, 96, 97, 133, 135 and 147.

[23]Ibid., p. 96.

[24]Ibid., p. 90. My case for emotions does not depend on the fusion theory. It would be just as strong even if the "add-on" theory were true, the theory that emotions contain two separate parts—feelings and cognitions. The fusion theory, however, is closer to our actual experiences of emotions, or so it seems to me.

If, then, emotions are both toned and cognitive, faith can be an emotion. As an emotion, faith would have an object and would therefore contain a perception of that object along with an assessment of the worth of the object, both of which are cognitive. The object, of course, would be God. And the emotion would be trust or some other emotion that satisfies the existential needs. Trust would be both toned and cognitive. It would not be blind, but would be aware of its object and would value it.

If faith is in part an emotion, the battle to keep one's faith would not always be between reason and emotion, with emotion undermining reason, as Lewis thought. It would just as often be between emotion and emotion, with one emotion undermining another—with love of admiration, for instance, undermining the emotion of trust. To say that the battle is always blind emotion subverting reason misconceives emotion and is inaccurate spiritual psychology.

Emotions are a substitute for action. In this last misconception of emotions, emotions are said to distract us from action. If all we do is feel, according to this view of emotions, we are likely to be so absorbed in our feelings that we do nothing when action is required. If faith were merely a feeling, it would be simply a "comforting sentiment, a druggy buzz into which one escapes to avoid reality," to use the words at the beginning of this chapter. Faith is, rather, a commitment, since commitment moves us to action.

The element of truth in this misconception of emotions is that emotions can, indeed, be substitutes for action and commitment, and even worse, can be a source of illusion. We might undergo intense emotions during a church service but do nothing when we walk out of the service. The emotions in this case delude us into thinking that we have an active and live faith.

This critique of emotion, however, has two faults. The first is that commitments fail to move us to action as often as emotions do. Commitments, as is well known, sometimes decrease in strength and so lose some of their moving power. This happens when desires that conflict with the commitments gain in strength. The conflicting desires then control our actions instead of the original commitments. So emotions are in no worse position than commitments in moving us to action.

And, second, emotions typically contain desires to act. In compassion, for example, our identification with someone's suffering makes us want to relieve that suffering. It would not be genuine compassion if we did not have this desire. Anger also contains desire. When we are angry at someone who has unjustifiably offended us, we want to express our feelings in some way. We may want to do something offensive in response or something that would redress our grievance in a just way. Emotions, in other words, typically contain action tendencies. They move us to action just as much as commitments do. Faith, then, can consist of emotion without compromising its own action tendency.

FAITH AS AN EMOTION

Dispelling these six critiques of emotion goes a long way toward conceiving of faith as an emotion. As an emotion, faith would remain stable and contribute to our well-being. It would be able to be cultivated and deepened. It would not be an independent part of our character, as is supposed by the emotion-versus-reason view, but would work with reason in various ways. And more can be said about emotion as a component of faith, beginning with additional thoughts about its connection to reason.

Tied to reason. As we saw, emotions (most of them, at any rate) are construals, or ways of seeing their objects. With faith in God, one construes reality in specific ways. One sees the physical universe as made by a personal being who cares for it. Because one regards the maker as good, one has confidence that in the end things will turn out well. The universe is ultimately a good place to be, one perceives.

Acquiring faith in God leads to new construals. If I have confidence that things will turn out well in the end, I will not regard tragedy as a crushing blow when it strikes me. I will suffer, to be sure, but I will not construe my suffering as totally incapacitating. In addition, if I have faith, I will more readily notice the emotional needs my acquaintances have and the difference faith in God could make in dealing with those needs. I will also recognize the appropriateness and goodness of a number of emotions, such as hope, humility and patience.

Because emotions are ways of seeing reality, they can be judged to be reasonable or unreasonable. Fear, for example, would be reasonable if it were based on an accurate assessment of danger, and anger would be unreasonable if it were disproportionate to the offense. Trust in someone would be appropriate if the person were reliable and judged worthy of being trusted. Faith in God, then, when conceived as trust, can be judged appropriate because of the reliability and worthiness of its object.

Embedded in a constellation of emotions. Emotions are not isolated. They are reinforced or diminished by other emotions. Anger, for example, is reinforced by impatience; those who are regularly impatient are likely to be more quickly angered. Anger is also reinforced by pride; those who think more highly of themselves than they ought to think are more likely to feel offended by unkind remarks about themselves. With patience and humility, though, anger is not so easily kindled. Trust in God is also affected by other emotions. With hope for a place beyond death that is free of turmoil and anxiety, one is more disposed to trust that God will bring about such a state. With awe of the enormous complexity of the universe and the even greater complexity of the cosmic mind that invented it, one is more disposed to trust that inventor. With enjoyment in the goodness of life, one finds it easier to trust the goodness of God. Those who easily get depressed by evil and pain, however, find it harder to acquire trust.

The constellation of emotions is like an intricately woven spider's web. At the center of the web there are roughly circular strands. They connect to the strands that form the spokes of the web, and the spokes are connected to each other by other strands. The whole web forms an elaborate network of grayish-silvery threads. If some of the strands of the web become broken, nearby strands sag. If too many of the spokes of the web become broken, the middle hangs down or it drops off entirely. Then the web becomes a motley conglomeration of broken threads. In us, the web is a complex system of emotions, desires, attitudes and thoughts. They depend on each other for their place in the web. If one of them becomes weak, closely connected ones also become weak. Faith is at or near the center of the web. If too many of the emotions on which faith depends dissolve, faith too dissolves. It requires other emotions to be sustained, and the other emotions require faith to survive. The center must hold or the whole system will fall apart.

That faith is embedded in a constellation of emotions means that cultivating faith is not simply a matter of working on an isolated emotion. Doing that would be difficult. When we cultivate emotions to which faith is connected, however, faith is affected as well. So one important strategy for working on deepening faith, when faith is conceived as an emotion, is to work on emotions to which faith is connected. It is not simply to reinforce reason, as the emotion-versus-reason paradigm would have it, though it may require that as well.

Involved in conversion. If faith is an emotion, it is involved in all the activities that faith is otherwise involved in, including conversion. In conversion, on the emotion conception of faith, one acquires an emotion that becomes the pivotal emotion in one's character—the emotion that gives a central focus to one's life and provides a unified aim for living. Acquiring this emotion changes many of the ways one construes events. It affects the emotions to which it is connected, intensifying some and inhibiting others. The emotion is what gives one energy and drive. It moves one to act in certain ways, think in certain ways and feel in certain ways. On the emotion view of faith, the strength of one's faith in God is measured not just by the intensity of the feeling in the emotion which constitutes the faith, as it is in the blind sensation conception of emotion critiqued above, but by the characteristics that the emotion has—its construals, its energy and its connections to reason and other emotions. The strength of one's faith is also measured by how well it satisfies the spiritual and emotional needs described in chapter two.

FAITH AND SATISFACTION OF NEED

The theme of this book is that though satisfaction of need cannot by itself justify faith in God, it can legitimately draw us to faith when it is conjoined with reason in one or more of the ways I have described. How, then, does faith connect to the satisfaction of need? The following simple argument is a distillation:

1. Faith in God consists partly of satisfaction of certain needs.

2. Satisfaction of these needs is an emotion.

3. Therefore, faith in God consists partly of an emotion.

When we satisfy the spiritual and emotional needs mentioned in the existential argument for believing in God, we have faith, and this faith is an emotion.

Faith in God consists partly of satisfaction of certain needs. If satisfaction of need is the origin of faith, then faith consists of satisfaction of those needs. A comparison to reason makes this evident. Suppose the reasons a person had for believing in God were the sole origin of their faith in God. These reasons might include a philosophical argument, an appeal to the miracles recorded in the Bible and perhaps C. S. Lewis's well-known argument that Jesus must be divine, all of which are evidential arguments.[25] If these arguments were what prompted someone to acquire faith, their faith would consist of assent, that is, a belief that God exists and that Jesus is who he said he was. The origin of faith determines what faith consists of. Thus, if satisfaction of need is the origin of faith in God, then faith in God consists of it. And if both satisfaction of need and evidential argumentation contribute to one's faith, then faith consists of both satisfaction of need and assent.

Satisfaction of these needs is an emotion. Again, it is not the satisfaction of just any need that is an emotion. If I need a doctor to look at a bone I think I have broken while out hiking in the mountains, the satisfaction of that need is not an emotion (though, of course, I may have various emotions when the need is satisfied). But meeting the need for cosmic security is an emotion because I have a feeling that construes reality in a certain way. I construe reality as a safe place to be, I construe God as making it safe, and I construe myself as dependent on God for my safety. And, of course, I feel safe. In addition, meeting my need for meaning by believing in God is an emotion. I construe God not simply as a vast energy that animates the galaxies but as a being that loves and feels. I believe that this being has made people for a purpose and that part of this purpose is to love well. And I feel something like safety in knowing that I am attempting to fulfill this purpose, along with a sense of inclusion in something larger than myself.

So, then, faith is partly an emotion. But this does not make faith

---

[25]For Lewis's argument, see *Mere Christianity*, pp. 51-52.

fickle or shallow, for emotions can be sturdy and profound. Nor does it make faith disconnected from reality or a refuge from life's hard realities, for emotions draw one to reality instead of detaching one from it, because they are construals and contain desires.

When faith is conceived of as being an emotion, it is tied to both need and reason. This makes it integrate with more parts of who we are than would be the case with just a need-based or reason-based conception of faith. As tied to need, faith satisfies the cravings that matter most to us, which makes it deeply comforting. As tied to reason, faith satisfies our need to be truly connected to what is real. This, too, is deeply comforting. Faith needs both kinds of comfort to be compelling.

AQUINAS AND KIERKEGAARD

The view that faith is partly an emotion can be located, too, in historical context. Thomas Aquinas and Søren Kierkegaard have views on faith that appear to be polar opposites. According to Aquinas, "faith denotes an assent of the understanding to what is believed,"[26] and according to Kierkegaard, "faith is the highest passion in a person."[27] What makes these assertions appear to be polar opposites is that for both Aquinas and Kierkegaard passion and understanding exclude each other. For Aquinas, beliefs do not contain passions, though, of course, the person who has beliefs may also have passions. The object of beliefs, says Aquinas is "truth."[28] But passions do not have truth as their objects, for they are neither true nor false. They just are. For Kierkegaard, beliefs are impersonal and objective, whereas passions are personal and subjective. The two are entirely different. Typical of his declarations on the incompatibility of faith and what is purely intellectual is this: "From the Christian point of view, faith belongs to the existential . . . and in all eternity it has nothing to do with knowledge."[29]

---

[26]Thomas Aquinas *Summa Theologica* II-II, Q 1, A 4, in *On Faith: Summa Theologica 2-2. qq. 1-16 of St. Thomas Aquinas*, trans. Mark D. Jordan (Notre Dame, Ind.: University of Notre Dame Press, 1990), p. 39.

[27]Søren Kierkegaard, *Fear and Trembling*, trans. Howard V. Hong and Edna H. Hong (Princeton: Princeton University Press, 1983), p. 122.

[28]Aquinas *Summa Theologica* II-II, Q 4, A 2, in *On Faith*, p. 107: "Believing is immediately an act of understanding, since the object of this act is truth."

[29]Søren Kierkegaard, *The Last Years: Journals 1853-55*, ed. and trans. Ronald Gregor Smith

We can call Aquinas's view the *belief view*, for it states that faith consists of true beliefs, such as that God exists, that God can be trusted and that God saves those who put their trust and hope in God. The central idea is that faith in God must actually be about God. This is what it means to say that the beliefs of which faith consists are true.

We can call Kierkegaard's view the *personal relationship view*, for it states that faith in God consists of a person-to-person connection. The central idea is that people connect to other persons via emotion and "passion" and not simply true beliefs. If the only connection a person had with another person was that the one had true beliefs about the other, it could hardly be called a friendship or love or trust or devotion. The two would not be connected as persons. But faith in God requires that one be connected to God as a person, which requires love, trust and devotion and, therefore, passion.

The reasons for each of these views of faith seem so obvious that they make one wonder whether Aquinas and Kierkegaard actually held what the other so rightly critiqued. Could they actually have held something closer to the other's view and not what the quotes I have given seem to indicate? As it happens, they say things that make their views less antagonistic.

Aquinas says that the assent which faith consists of is produced "by a choice of the will."[30] It is the "will" that "moves it [the understanding] to assent."[31] So, according to Aquinas, when one has faith, one also has willing. This act of willing the assent, the choice a person makes to believe true things about God, is not impersonal and objective. If someone assented to true statements about God solely because the statements had good evidence in their favor, there would be no choice. The assent would be impersonal and objective. But, Aquinas states, there is more than just evidence that produces the assent. There is willing.

There is also charity. Aquinas states, "Charity is called the form of faith, inasmuch as the act of faith is completed and formed by charity."[32]

(New York: Harper & Row, 1965), pp. 99-100.
[30]Aquinas *Summa Theologica* II-II, Q 1, A 4, in *On Faith*, p. 40.
[31]Ibid., Q 4, A 2, p. 107.
[32]Ibid., Q 4, A 3, p. 109.

Aquinas knows that bare believing is impersonal and objective. But when charity is added to bare believing—or, to use Aquinas's words, when the believing is formed by charity—it comes to life. The person who assents connects to God as one person connects to another, and not simply as one who knows true things about the other. There are, then, for Aquinas three components of the inner state that connects one to God: assent, willing and charity. And in the combination of these we have something with which Kierkegaard would have been more satisfied. If Aquinas had called the combination of these three faith, instead of limiting faith just to assent, then that would have been more a terminological difference with Kierkegaard than a substantive one.

Kierkegaard, too, says things that make his personal relationship view of faith closer to Aquinas's belief view. Scattered throughout his books are statements about God that he believes are true. He believes that God forgives sin, that God's grace is the only means of salvation and numerous other Christian claims.[33] Kierkegaard does not provide a systematic treatment of these claims, for his aim was to incite people who already believed them to acquire genuine faith. He thought that churchgoers in nineteenth-century Denmark did not have the passion that connecting to God as a person requires. They merely had true beliefs about God. But, again, having true beliefs about God is not enough, he thought, to be rightly connected to God. That is why he insisted that faith is a passion, the highest passion a person can have.

To make his point, Kierkegaard exaggerated. He declared that "truth is subjectivity" and that one could be "in the truth" even if one were passionately connected to what is objectively false.[34] He said that faith has nothing to do with knowledge. He exaggerated because he thought that those who believed they were rightly connected to God because of their beliefs about God were blinded by those beliefs. He thought, in fact, that they were trying to evade God by having the beliefs. More accurately, the true source of the evasion was having the same beliefs as

---

[33]For an extensive treatment of biblical references in Kierkegaard's writings, see L. Joseph Rosas III, *Scripture in the Thought of Søren Kierkegaard* (Nashville: Broadman & Holman, 1994).

[34]Søren Kierkegaard, *Concluding Unscientific Postscript*, trans. Howard V. Hong and Edna H. Hong (Princeton: Princeton University Press, 1992), 1:199.

everyone else in nineteenth-century Denmark. It was merely a "crowd faith," not a genuine connection to God. Kierkegaard gets at the connection between having a crowd faith and evasion: "The most pernicious of all evasions is—hidden in the crowd, to want, as it were, to avoid God's inspection of oneself as a single individual, avoid hearing God's voice as a single individual."[35] His point is that when people are in a crowd, they uncritically take on the beliefs of the crowd without making them their own and thereby use the crowd to hide from God. This means that one cannot get churchgoers to have genuine faith simply by preaching the right beliefs to them. They already have those beliefs. What has to be done is to exaggerate and diagnose and perhaps even pretend that one is not oneself a Christian by writing under pseudonyms. Kierkegaard did all of these.[36] The exaggerations, unfortunately, make it look as if the only component of the inner state of connection to God is bare passion. But Kierkegaard definitely believes that part of that inner state consists of believing true things about God. Two such beliefs appear in the evasion quote just given: God inspects people and God speaks to people. Kierkegaard did not, however, include these true beliefs in what he typically calls faith, just as Aquinas did not include willing and charity in his definition of faith. But both are nevertheless in a person who connects rightly to God.

So, then, what Aquinas and Kierkegaard believed about people who have faith is not as antagonistic as their statements about faith seem to indicate. This, of course, does not mean that their views are the same. For Aquinas the central focus of faith is true belief, and for Kierkegaard it is passion. They represent two major traditions in Christian thinking about faith.

---

[35] Kierkegaard, *Upbuilding Discourses in Various Spirits*, p. 128. Quoted more fully in chapter six, "Obstacles," p. 117.

[36] For more on the interpretation of Kierkegaard I employ in this paragraph, see the books and articles of C. Stephen Evans, especially *Passionate Reason: Making Sense of Kierkegaard's Philosophical Fragments* (Bloomington: Indiana University Press, 1992), *Faith Beyond Reason: A Kierkegaardian Account* (Grand Rapids: Eerdmans, 1998), *Kierkegaard: On Faith and the Self* (Waco, Tex.: Baylor University Press, 2006), and "Is Kierkegaard an Irrationalist? Reason, Paradox, and Faith," *Religious Studies* 25 (September, 1989): 347-62. See also Kierkegaard's *On My Work as an Author* and *The Point of View for My Work as an Author*, in *The Point of View*, trans. Howard V. Hong and Edna H. Hong (Princeton: Princeton University Press, 1998).

My view, that faith is partly an emotion, does not fit well with the belief view, at least not in the exclusive way I originally presented Aquinas's position. To belief I add satisfaction of need. The needs described in chapter two are an essential part of what humans are, and a faith that ignores them is deficient. The belief view has generally ignored needs, except, of course, the need to know what is true. In so doing, it has overintellectualized faith and misperceived what humans really are. Humans are at least as much creatures with existential needs as creatures with minds. Faith must include the satisfaction of those needs.

My view is closer to Kierkegaard's view of faith, provided it contains the conception of emotions I have put forth. Though Kierkegaard does not systematically treat the subject, he does make scattered comments indicating that he may in fact hold to something like it.[37] Whatever view he actually holds, though, emotion needs to be supplemented with beliefs about God in addition to the construals that the emotions themselves contain. The personal relationship view, in rightly pointing out the centrality of needs and emotions, often ignores the role of the mind in acquiring and maintaining faith. In so doing, it has overemotionalized faith. Minds, though, are an essential part of what humans are, and a faith that ignores them is deficient. Humans are at least as much creatures with minds as creatures with emotions and needs. Faith, then, must include beliefs, both those involved with emotions and additional ones involving God.

---

[37]For a defense of the view that Kierkegaard held to a cognitive view of emotions, see Robert C. Roberts, "Existence, Emotion, and Virtue: Classical Themes in Kierkegaard," in *The Cambridge Companion to Kierkegaard*, ed. Alastair Hannay and Gordon D. Marino (Cambridge: Cambridge University Press, 1998), pp. 177-206.

9

PURSUING FAITH

Miguel de Unamuno, a Spanish philosopher, wrote, "It is the ardent longing that there may be a God who guarantees the eternity of consciousness that leads us to believe in him."[1] This quote captures the essence of the existential argument for believing in God:

1. We have an ardent longing for a God who guarantees the eternity of consciousness.

2. Believing in a God who guarantees the eternity of consciousness satisfies this longing.

The inference from these two assertions, which Unamuno does not state, but which he appears to endorse, is,

3. Therefore, we are justified in believing in this God.

I have conceded to the four objections that this argument does not work. Need by itself does not justify believing in God. However, when need is supplemented with reason in some way, then need does legitimately draw us to faith in God. This drawing leads to the following three claims: we should let ourselves be drawn to faith by need, we often do not, and part of what makes life so spectacular are the emotions we have when we satisfy our existential needs with faith in God.

---

[1]Miguel de Unamuno, *Tragic Sense of Life*, trans. J. E. Crawford Flitch (New York: Dover Publications, 1954), p. 186.

DRAWN TO FAITH IN GOD BY NEED

We should let ourselves be drawn to faith in God by need is a moral claim. This book's thesis—the ideal way to acquire and sustain faith is through need and reason—is an epistemic claim, one dealing with how faith can be secure. But using need to acquire faith also has moral value. We *should* let ourselves be drawn to faith in God by need because doing so produces desirable emotions. And a life with more desirable emotions in it is better than one with fewer of them or without them altogether.

Desirable emotions. The emotions that satisfy our existential needs are desirable partly because they are intrinsically good and partly because they have good effects. For emotions to be intrinsically good means that there is nothing else that makes them good. They are end-of-the-line goods. Consider a couple examples.

Delighting in goodness is evoked when we observe, then esteem and revere, some good activity or condition. The delight is good whether or not it has any effects on us or anyone else. It is good to delight in someone's good character or activity "just because." The same is true of awe. The reverential wonder evoked when we think of the grandeur of God is good regardless of what the awe does to us.

Delight and awe are also good because they produce in us the disposition to look for more goodness and grandeur. They cause us to open up to love or the longing for heaven and to be more convinced of the value of doing so. And when we express our delight and awe to others, we are doing something that is both intrinsically good and good because of what our expression does to those others.

Is there a way of showing that religious emotions are intrinsically good? Unfortunately, showing that anything is intrinsically good is notoriously difficult, and it would take us too far afield to treat the matter adequately. One imaginative technique, nonetheless, appears to show that religious emotions are intrinsically good. Imagine a world without any emotions. In this world, the highest creatures would be plants and animals (those, at least, that do not have emotions), or perhaps Mr. Spocks—creatures who look like humans but who are devoid of feeling and emotion. We would, I believe, regard such a world as having less value than the one we inhabit. It would be barren and desolate, even if it were filled with beauty and other natural goods, for the Mr. Spocks would not be able to appreciate these goods. We would not want to be a Mr. Spock in this world, nor would we want others to be that way either, for we want emotions both for ourselves and for others so that we can connect to them via emotions. This is because we regard emotions as being intrinsically good.

Now imagine a world in which there are emotions, but not any of those that are connected to the needs mentioned in the existential argument for believing in God. There would be no awe, meaning, delight in goodness or sense of cosmic security. The humanlike creatures in this world would be only minimal humans—"people" who could feel some emotions but not others. They might be able to feel fear or devotion to a cause, but not moral or religious emotions. This new world would not be as barren or desolate as the first one, but we would still sense it as deficient. It would be without something that we value as necessary to a good and full life.

A better life. If, then, the emotions that satisfy the needs mentioned in the existential argument for believing in God are intrinsically good, and if they have good effects, our lives will have more worth if we have them than if we do not. Our lives will be richer and larger. This is why we should let ourselves be drawn to faith in God by means of need—because when we have such faith, we have emotions that give our lives more overall value. God, of course, designed it this way. Because God values emotions, and in particular, those connected to the needs mentioned in the existential argument for believing in God, God made us to be the kind of creatures who could have them and not Mr. Spocks or minimal humans with only a small range of emotions. We would have a diminished existence if we did not possess any religious emotions, possessed only a few of them or did not experience them fully.

These thoughts can be derived from connecting two verses in the New Testament. In John 10:10, Jesus says he came so that people can have life "abundantly." An abundant life is one that has overall worth, which means that it possesses the values that the New Testament enunciates. Some of these values are listed in Galatians 5:22-23 as features of those who have "the Spirit"—love, joy, peace, patience, kindness, generosity, faithfulness, gentleness and self-control. An abundant life contains, then, as many of these features as possible. Since some or all of them are emotions, the abundant life that Jesus offers consists partly of having certain emotions. And since emotions are derived from needs, the abundant life consists partly of satisfying certain needs. If the needs were not satisfied and we did not have the emotions, we would not have the abundant life Jesus offers. Our life would be narrow and constricted, having less overall worth than it could have.

Caring about needs. We should, then, care about whether we experience awe or delight in goodness or let ourselves be loved by God. One of our driving passions should be that our lives be abundant. We should pay attention to our restlessness, to the obstacles we erect to avoid satisfying existential needs with faith in God, to the value of the emotions that satisfy these needs and to whether these emotions are really satisfying to us.

Pascal was appalled at those who do not care about matters involving their connection to God. Of those who do care about such matters but who remain skeptical even though they have expended much energy in trying to discover the truth about God, he wrote, "I can feel nothing but compassion for those who sincerely lament their doubt, who regard it as the ultimate misfortune, and who, sparing no effort to escape from it, make their search their principal and most serious business."[2] But he regarded those who are not concerned about their connection to God differently. "As for those who spend their lives without a thought for this final end of life, . . . I view them very differently. This negligence in a matter where they themselves, their eternity, their all are at stake, fills me more with irritation than pity; it astounds and appalls me; it seems quite monstrous to me."[3] Pascal was appalled because he thought that matters involving our connection to God have overriding importance: "The immortality of the soul is something of such vital importance to us, affecting us so deeply, that one must have lost all feeling not

---

[2]Blaise Pascal, *Pensées*, trans. A. J. Krailsheimer (New York: Penguin Books, 1995), #427 (p. 129).
[3]Ibid.

to care about knowing the facts of the matter."[4] We should not shrug our shoulders at something that has such significance.

Those who do not shrug their shoulders at their existential and emotional needs expend energy in efforts to satisfy them at least as much as they do in efforts to satisfy other needs. They are drawn to people who display the same energy. The character trait they have is, straightforwardly, caring for one's own needs. All those whose faith journeys appear in this book have this trait to a high degree. They have pursued faith with much concern.

Such people should not be considered self-absorbed or self-preoccupied. As I pointed out in chapter two, some existential needs are other-directed, such as the need to love or delight in goodness. Moreover, the aim of satisfying the self-directed needs is not simply to get something for oneself. It is about living well. To use Jesus' words again, it is about having an abundant life, one that is not meager or emaciated. And since God put the needs into us, wanting to satisfy them is about living as God designed us to live.

Like acquiring friends. Miguel de Unamuno gives a hint about how we can let ourselves be drawn to faith in God through satisfaction of needs. He says, "I believe in God as I believe in my friends, because I feel the breath of his affection, feel his invisible and intangible hand, drawing me, leading me, grasping me."[5] We are drawn to God in the same ways we are drawn to friends, Unamuno says, namely, through satisfying our need for affection and intimacy. If, then, we should let ourselves be drawn to faith in God, we should cultivate these ways. We should think about the distinctive means by which we have been drawn to our friends and then consciously use these means to acquire or deepen faith in God.

Unamuno tells us a couple of ways this can be done. We can let ourselves feel someone's affection, and we can let ourselves feel the ways in which they "grasp" us, that is, the ways that show they want to connect to us. To these we can add more: we can let ourselves feel the affirmation a friend has expressed and their acceptance of us in spite of our

---

[4]Ibid., #427 (p. 128).
[5]Unamuno, *Tragic Sense of Life*, p. 194.

blunders. We can notice the little kindnesses they extend to us and the gratitude we have for those kindnesses. If Unamuno correctly declares that we acquire faith in God in the same way we acquire friends, then it is but a short step from the latter to the former.

Acquiring friends, however, does not occur only by means of satisfaction of need. If so, it would succumb to the same objections that the existential argument for believing in God succumbs to. Friendships must occur by means of need and reason. And this is what actually happens.

Imagine that we meet someone who displays affection toward us. She wants to be with us, likes talking to us and parts with a kiss. She is, however, an extortionist, one who blackmails people whose vulnerabilities she uncovers. Eventually she hints that she wants us to join her in a scheme she is concocting. If affection were the only characteristic that drew us to her and keeps us connected, we would remain friends. But reason kicks in and rejects her values and, with that, probably the friendship. Actually, reason has already been employed in weighing her values and coming to trust her. It has seen that being with her and receiving her affection fit with what we want to do with our lives. It has also seen that she handles our confidences with trustworthiness. Both need and reason, then, draw us to her. So Unamuno's suggestion about how we acquire friends and faith must be unpacked so as to include both.

WHEN NEEDS DO NOT DRAW US TO GOD

But sometimes we do not let ourselves be drawn to faith in God by need. That is, we do not always do so, do not often do so or, perhaps, never do so. How does this happen, and why?

Ways we do not let ourselves be drawn to faith in God by need. Here are three such ways. First, we let other needs crowd out the needs mentioned in the existential argument. We put our energy into satisfying those other needs instead of the existential needs. The other needs are, to be sure, genuinely good and so must be satisfied. But we let them dominate our care and concern. Second, we let numerous everyday activities eclipse satisfaction of the existential needs. Doing these activities is, again, good, but they cause us not to think about the existential needs. Third, we focus on reason as a way of knowing God or proving God or defending belief in God against objections. Here, too, reason is good and, indeed, necessary. But we use it to avoid connecting to God through satisfaction of need.

Kierkegaard pounced on this last point. He thought that church-goers in nineteenth-century Denmark used reason as a way of evading God. "All this interpreting and reinterpreting and scholarly research and new scholarly research that is produced on the solemn and serious principle that it is to understand God's Word properly—look more closely and you will see that it is to defend oneself against God's Word. It is only all too easy to understand the requirement contained in God's Word."[6] Kierkegaard recommends the religious psychoanalysis I described in chapter six as the proper way of looking more closely. He was trying to find the real motives for a religious person's use of reason. It may be, of course, that such a person is honestly trying to find out what is true about God and not trying to hide from God. Still, Kierkegaard thought, we humans are so relentless in our attempts to hide from God and so adroit at finding ways of doing so that we often use reason to hide from God. We use what is good to evade what is good.

Reasons for not letting ourselves be drawn to faith in God by need. These reasons are the same as the cognitive and noncognitive obstacles that prevent us from seeing that we have the existential needs in the first place. These include the cognitive obstacle of not seeing clearly how faith in God would satisfy the needs better than a nonfaith state. We are not too sure what faith is, perhaps, or not sure why we need it in addition to simple human love or delight in human goodness. The obstacles also include the noncognitive ones of pride and self-preoccupation, which cause us not to want to satisfy the needs with faith in God. We resist faith in God because we see that we would have to give up the self-concern that so occupies our energy and the autonomy that we prize. We do not want to let go of the dear self, so we are blinded to the value of faith in God.

A good deal more could be said about the psychology of resistance—

---

[6]Søren Kierkegaard, *For Self-Examination*, trans. Howard V. Hong and Edna H. Hong (Princeton: Princeton University Press, 1990), p. 34.

and much has—but here it must suffice simply to mention its role in obscuring needs that lead to faith in God.

EMOTIONS FOR LIFE

What makes life so spectacular? The emotions do. Imagine not having emotions while doing something breathtaking and striking, such as hiking to the top of a mountain or approaching a port in a faraway country on a cruise around the world. It would be a very flat experience. The anticipation, exhilaration and awe are what make these experiences valuable to us. The same is true of everyday experiences, such as finishing a task, seeing a loved one again after an interval or thinking about some fascinating topic. Part of what we like about finishing a task is the pride (in the good sense) that accompanies it, the sense that we have done something good. Part of what we like about seeing someone we love at the end of a workday or after months of separation is the renewed sentiment of caring for and connecting with the person. Part of what we like about thinking about a fascinating topic is the excitement in exploring something new. To be sure, the task, the connecting and the exploring themselves have value. But emotions must accompany them if they are to be the grand and magnificent events that they are. (Nothing is ordinary. Everything is magical.)

Emotions also make God's life spectacular, if we can speak of God having a life. God is not a cosmic Mr. Spock. God does not spin out the universe just via intelligence. If God did, then God's life would be narrow and flat. But God's life is the most abundant possible. That is, God's life exemplifies all possible values consistent with being a perfect being. Though God does not have courage or fear, because these spring from finitude, God does delight in goodness and beauty and obtains satisfaction from loving and being loved. These are part of what makes God's existence so magnificent and awe-evoking, and, therefore, ours, too, since we have been made in God's image.

If, then, emotions make human life so spectacular, then so do the emotions that satisfy the needs mentioned in the existential argument for believing in God. When these are cultivated, we will feel that magnificence. We will feel that life is good and wonderful.

We humans find ourselves with certain deep and abiding needs. We don't know why we have them. Yet they are present in us, calling for a response. We need to love, so we love. We need meaning, so we do meaningful things. We need to kneel, so we kneel.

FOR FURTHER READING

Bishop, John. *Believing by Faith: An Essay in the Epistemology and Ethics of Religious Belief.* Oxford: Clarendon, 2007.

Callahan, Sidney. *In Good Conscience: Reason and Emotion in Moral Decision Making.* New York: HarperSanFrancisco, 1991.

Corrigan, John, Eric Crump and John Kloos. *Emotion and Religion: A Critical Assessment and Annotated Bibliography.* Westport, Conn.: Greenwood Press, 2000.

Elliott, Matthew A. *Faithful Feelings: Rethinking Emotion in the New Testament.* Grand Rapids: Kregel, 2006.

Evans, C. Stephen. "Kierkegaard and Plantinga on Belief in God: Subjectivity as the Ground of Properly Basic Religious Beliefs." *Faith and Philosophy* 5 (January 1988): 25-39.

Goldie, Peter. *The Emotions: A Philosophical Exploration.* Oxford: Clarendon, 2000.

Helm, Paul, ed. *Faith and Reason.* New York: Oxford University Press, 1999.

James, William. "Faith and the Right to Believe." In *The Writings of William James*, pp. 735-39. Edited by John J. McDermott. New York: Modern Library, 1968.

———. "The Sentiment of Rationality." In *The Writings of William James*, pp. 317-45. Edited by John J. McDermott. New York: Modern Library, 1968.

———. "The Will to Believe." In *The Writings of William James*, pp. 717-35. Edited by John J. McDermott. New York: Modern Library, 1968.

Järveläinen, Petri. *A Study on Religious Emotions.* Helsinki: Luther-Agricola-Society, 2000.

Lester, Andrew D. "Thinking About Emotion." In *The Angry Christian: A Theology for Care and Counseling*, pp. 19-63. Louisville: Westminster John Knox Press, 2003.

Lewis, C. S. *Mere Christianity*. New York: HarperCollins, 2001.

Lynch, Michael P. *True to Life: Why Truth Matters*. Cambridge, Mass.: MIT Press, 2004.

McGrath, Gavin, W. C. Campbell-Jack and C. Stephen Evans, eds. *New Dictionary of Christian Apologetics*. Downers Grove, Ill.: InterVarsity Press, 2006.

Meiland, Jack. "What Ought We to Believe? or the Ethics of Belief Revisited." In *The Theory of Knowledge: Classical and Contemporary Readings*, pp. 514-25. Edited by Louis P. Pojman. Belmont, Calif.: Wadsworth, 1993. Originally published in *American Philosophical Quarterly* 17 (1980): 15-24.

Mitchell, Basil. *The Justification of Religious Belief*. New York: Oxford University Press, 1981.

Moser, Paul. *The Elusive God: Reorienting Religious Epistemology*. New York: Cambridge University Press, 2008.

Newman, Jay. "Cardinal Newman's 'Factory-Girl Argument.'" *Proceedings of the American Catholic Philosophical Association* 46 (1972): 71-77.

Newman, John Henry. *The Grammar of Assent*. Garden City, N.Y.: Image Books, 1955.

Nussbaum, Martha C. *Upheavals of Thought: The Intelligence of Emotions*. Cambridge: Cambridge University Press, 2001.

Pascal, Blaise. *Pensées*. Translated by A. J. Krailsheimer. New York: Penguin Books, 1995.

Pojman, Louis. *Religious Belief and the Will*. New York: Routledge & Kegan Paul, 1986.

Roberts, Robert C. *Emotions: An Essay in Aid of Moral Psychology*. Cambridge: Cambridge University Press, 2003.

———. *Spiritual Emotions: A Psychology of Christian Virtues*. Grand Rapids: Eerdmans, 2007.

Solomon, Robert C. *The Passions: Emotions and the Meaning of Life*. Garden City, N.Y.: Indianapolis: Hackett, 1993.

———. *True to Our Feelings: What Our Emotions Are Really Telling Us*. New York: Oxford University Press, 2007.

———, ed. *What Is an Emotion? Classic and Contemporary Readings*, 2nd ed. New York: Oxford University Press, 2003.

Stoker, Wessel. *Is Faith Rational: A Hermeneutical-Phenomenological Accounting for Faith*. Dudley, Mass.: Peeters, 2006.

Swinburne, Richard. *Faith and Reason,* 2nd ed. Oxford: Clarendon, 2005.

Unamuno, Miguel de. *Tragic Sense of Life*. Translated by J. E. Crawford Flitch. New York: Dover Publications, 1954.

Wainwright, William J. *Reason and the Heart: A Prolegomenon to a Critique of Passional Reason*. Ithaca, N.Y.: Cornell University Press, 1995.

Wright, N. T. *Simply Christian: Why Christianity Makes Sense*. New York: HarperSanFrancisco, 2006.

Wynn, Mark R. *Emotional Experience and Religious Understanding: Integrating Perception, Conception and Feeling*. Cambridge: Cambridge University Press, 2005.

Index